D0442522

A WOMAN'S GUIDE TO BREAKING BONDAGES

A Woman's Guide to Breaking Bondages

Quin Sherrer and
Ruthanne Garlock

Servant Publications
Ann Arbor, Michigan

Vine books is an imprint of Servant Publications
especially designed to serve evangelical Christians.

Published by Servant Publications
P.O. Box 8617
Ann Arbor, Michigan 48107

The circumstances of certain events and some names of persons and locations have been changed to protect individuals' privacy.

Cover design by Multnomah Graphics/Printing
Cover illustration by Krieg Barrie
Text design by Diane Bareis

Printed in the United States of America
ISBN 0-89283-845-0

ACKNOWLEDGMENTS

Dedicated to our wonderful intercessors who covered us with prayer as we wrote, especially to:

Pastor Dutch Sheets and his congregation at Springs Harvest Fellowship in Colorado Springs, Colorado, who were diligent prayer warriors for us.

The intercessors of the Spiritual Warfare Network headed by Bobbye Byerly, Bill Anderson, and Chuck Pierce.

Numerous others—Cindy Finberg, Ann Rosenberg, Beth Alves, Cindy Jacobs, Keren Stoll, Rose Barton, JoAnne Bailey, Fran Ewing, Pat Haynes, Linda Martines, and Quin's children (Quinett, Keith and Dana, Sherry and Kim).

To the women who allowed us to share their stories of pain and victory to encourage you on your journey to freedom.

To our husbands, LeRoy Sherrer and John Garlock, who prayed earnestly for us during this project and gave us the time and space needed to write.

OTHER BOOKS BY THE AUTHORS

How to Pray for Your Children
by Quin Sherrer

How to Forgive Your Children
How to Pray for Your Family and Friends
A Woman's Guide to Spiritual Warfare
The Spiritual Warrior's Prayer Guide
by Quin Sherrer and Ruthanne Garlock

A House of Many Blessings
by Quin Sherrer and Laura Watson

Before We Kill and Eat You
Fire in His Bones
by Ruthanne Garlock

The Christian in Complete Armour (three volumes)
Ruthanne Garlock was the senior editor for the abridged edition of this Puritan classic written by William Gurnall in 1655.

Contents

INTRODUCTION

As hundreds of Christian women—many of them readers of our books—have asked us for help with their struggles, we've noticed these as some of their major bondages:

- low self-esteem
- negative or pessimistic thinking
- guilt
- anger
- doubt and unbelief
- fear
- grief and disappointment
- unforgiveness
- occult involvement
- addictive behavior
- illicit sexual activity
- aftermath of abuse
- rejection and shame
- generational influences

Have you allowed Satan to keep you in bondage and you don't know how to get free? Have you prayed about your problem without seeing results? Have you fought waves of hopelessness that you could ever be free? This book will provide guidelines in finding your way out of that maze through the enabling power of the

Holy Spirit. It will teach you how to have spiritual discernment and how to focus on Jesus, the life-giver, rather than on Satan, the father of lies.

The stories of those who have found freedom, and their steps out of bondage, will be a personal help and encouragement to women who wish to get free and stay free. You will feel their pain, identify with their battles, and rejoice in their victories. Our sisterhood in Christ is both valuable and powerful; we encourage you to use these guidelines in ministering to other women.

This book is a follow-up to two of our previous books, *A Woman's Guide to Spiritual Warfare* and *The Spiritual Warrior's Prayer Guide* (Servant), both of which we encourage you to read.

—Quin Sherrer and
Ruthanne Garlock

ONE

What Is Bondage? How Does It Occur?

Now after you have known God, or rather are known by God, how is it that you turn again to the weak and beggarly elements, to which you desire again to be in bondage? Galatians 4:9, NKJV

Are you a woman trying to cope with chronic depression, outbursts of anger, an addiction, a painful marriage, or a broken relationship? Do you feel weighed down, as if problem after problem is stacked on your shoulders so you can hardly stand?

In a word, *are you in bondage?* How did it happen? Certainly not overnight. No, the problem increased its grip on you, tightening slowly like a vise. Surely, had you known how to break its hold, you would have.

The good news is Jesus came to set the captives free! You need not remain in that bondage which harasses you and steals your joy.

Just the other day, over sandwiches at a small cafe, an attractive young woman I'd recently met asked me (Quin) to pray for her because her once-close relationship with the Lord was waning. She couldn't even identify her bondage. As we prayed, deep-seated fear was exposed. Fear so strong it kept her from trusting anyone, even God. That day, she took the first baby steps out of bondage by confessing her fear and asking God for his help. Even to pray again was a major breakthrough.

Although the enemy will oppose and try to obstruct your release, as my friend experienced, he cannot stop you if you truly want to be free. Even since becoming a Christian, you may feel that invisible chains are hindering your walk of freedom. Breaking these bondages does not guarantee you will have a problem-free life. But it does mean you are at last empowered by Christ to confront life's problems and overcome them.

The goal of this book is to help Christian women struggling with bondages, and to steer them toward freedom.

ARE YOU BONDAGE-PRONE?

While women are greatly valued in the kingdom of God, Satan, our adversary, is bent on hindering our ability to get free—and stay free—in Christ Jesus.

Do you sometimes feel:

- that you're never truly accepted by others—that you never seem to measure up to the woman you think you ought to be?
- that you absolutely can never forgive that certain someone who has wounded you so badly?
- afraid that your secret addictions to such things as romance novels, TV soap operas, shopping, over-the-counter drugs, alcohol, and so forth might be discovered?
- fearful that twisted beliefs and behaviors in your "family's history" have a grip on you?
- that you are so prone to anger you are sometimes ashamed to call yourself a Christian?
- that eating disorders have you in captivity?
- that you are driven by sexual temptations?

- that unresolved grief, disappointment, or guilt have ensnared you?
- that your former occult activity still affects your life?

Maybe you thought that the moment you became a Christian you'd be instantly free of all bondages that seemed to bind you. No more a slave to a sin or habit that had troubled you for so long. No more struggle with your conscience between right and wrong.

Amazing as it seems, some people prefer bondage over freedom—judging by their tendency to fall back into their old ways. The verse at the beginning of this chapter reveals Paul's concern that Christians who had been set free from the bondage of heathen religions now were being bound by Jewish law and religious tradition. The truth is, we human beings are bondage-prone—even though freedom is available.

Perhaps you learned this Scripture when you accepted Jesus as Savior: "Therefore, if anyone is in Christ, he is a new creation; old things have passed away; behold, all things have become new" (2 Cor 5:17, NKJV).

Yet you quickly discovered that the "become new" part is not instantaneous. Yes, the minute you confess, repent of your sin, and seek God's forgiveness, you receive salvation and cleansing by the blood of Jesus. In that sense "old things"—the official record of your sin and rebellion against God—"pass away." The root word in Greek means "to perish." Your sin literally is wiped from the record and you are now born again, a member of the family of God.

FLESH VS. SPIRIT

But then you begin to struggle with the conflict between your wonderful new way of life in Christ and the magnetic pull of worldly thoughts and ways from your former life. Satan plants doubts in your mind and temptations on your path—you discover his fingerprints are still on many areas of your life. Some of those "old things" from the past hinder your progress in following God's ways and becoming new. How can you break free?

The last part of that verse—"all things have become new"—means "the old thoughts of God and of sin and salvation have received fresh colouring—they are 'become new.'"[1]

In other words, when you receive Christ as Savior, your mind becomes renewed. Your understanding of God goes through a process of change, as well as your perception of yourself, the world, and how you operate in it.

We could compare this process of walking free with what happens when a refugee flees his own country, which is ruled by a cruel dictator, and finds acceptance in a free country. Recognizing the bondage of despotism and burning with a desire to be rid of it, he runs to freedom. Many of his fellow citizens in the land of bondage choose to remain there.

But adapting to a new way of life and even a new language in the land of freedom—while getting rid of the old thought patterns and behaviors—takes time. Some refugees adapt more quickly than others; some carry a lot of "baggage" from their former way of life that needs to be eliminated. The flesh, the "sinful nature," must be put to death and not permitted to act as we choose to live by the Spirit. Paul wrote: "Those who live according to the sinful nature have their minds set on what that nature desires; but those who live in accordance with the Spirit have their minds set on what the Spirit desires" (Rom 8:5).

Each of us comes to Christ from a different background and culture, and at varying levels of maturity. The progressive steps and the timetable of truly "becoming new" will be different for each individual. And for some, specific areas of bondage need to be addressed.

What, exactly, is bondage? In a nutshell, it is involuntary servitude or slavery. Someone who is in bondage is: dominated, restrained, usually by compulsion, subjugated to a controlling person or force.

Paul writes that before receiving Christ we "followed the ways of this world and of the ruler of the kingdom of the air..." (Eph 2:2b). That ruler is Satan, and his emissaries are demons or evil spirits. We literally were under Satan's rulership—or in bondage to him—whether consciously aware of it or not. Our freedom through Christ breaks that bondage, but we still have the power of choice. We can choose to yield to temptation and cooperate with demonic influences, but the Holy Spirit is available to help strengthen us to stand against Satan's temptations.

BONDAGE INDICATORS

Bible teacher Dean Sherman defines bondage as it applies to a Christian:

> If we continue in a habit of sin, we can develop a bondage. A bondage means that there is a supernatural element to our problem. The enemy now has a grip on a function of our personality. Traditionally, we have talked of a progression, with people being obsessed, oppressed, or possessed. But I have stopped using these words because it is hard to define where one stops and another begins. The word "possessed" doesn't appear in original Scriptures; the word used is simply "demonized." That is what I am calling a bondage. It is possible to have a bondage that does not consume your entire personality and function—you are merely bound in a certain part of your personality. Whatever the bondage, and whatever the degree, if you are bound, you need to be set free in Jesus' name.[2]

And what are the indicators that bondage exists in a believer's life? Following are some of the bondages our readers have written us about. You may see yourself or a loved one in these excerpts.

- I don't drink or smoke—just compulsively overeat. I want to overcome this sin. Please help me.
- I said "No" to marriage to my former fiancé—who was involved in a cult—unless he accepted Jesus. I really want to go

on with my life, but I am still consumed with thoughts of him and want him back.

- I've had several abortions. I don't believe that God will ever forgive me.
- I envision God as someone who makes things very hard, then waits for me to goof so he can punish me.
- Since my husband left me for another woman, I've decided that I can never trust any man again.
- My childhood memories of abuse are very painful and I don't know how to deal with them. I either bottle up my emotions, or cry like I am out of control.
- I have lived with much guilt and shame and have never admitted to anyone my affair with a deacon in our church.
- For years I was a compulsive liar and thief. I thought when I became a Christian I would be free of these compulsions, but they tempt me constantly.
- I do not feel strong enough to battle the evil forces that are destroying the lives of my family.

HOW DOES BONDAGE OCCUR?

The "how" of bondage has no easy answer which applies in every situation. Each of our lives has different circumstances which influence how we view God, ourselves, and the world. And each of us has one or more weak points where the enemy seeks to gain a foothold. It is in these areas of weakness that bondages are most likely to develop.

Maybe you've struggled with some of the same weaknesses as Lori, who had a close relationship with the Lord until she became a working mother and her circumstances began to overwhelm her.

For nights on end she got up hour after hour to tend a crying baby. Arriving at the office the next morning fatigued, she boiled inside when her boss yelled at her. In the evening her husband, exhausted from his own demanding job, complained about dinner being burned. She would do the dishes, two loads of laundry, then fall into bed after everyone else—only to get up several more times in the night to soothe a crying child.

As many of us are prone to do, Lori ignored the frustration and anger building up inside her as she struggled just to keep up with all the demands facing her every day. She took no time for prayer in the morning before rushing the baby to the sitter, then dashing to the office. But soon that buried anger began to surface. She found herself yelling at her baby and her husband, and biting her tongue to keep from screaming back at her boss.

Over the weeks and months Lori slipped into a bondage to anger and self-pity. She longed for her carefree days as a single career gal. She even fantasized about writing a hateful note and running away. Yet, if you asked Lori, she'd say, "Of course I'm a Christian! I'm in church every Sunday with my family." But in a secret place of her heart, that reservoir of anger had given the enemy a foothold by which to bring her into the grip of bondage.

Do you see how the enemy was at work here and how Lori's bondage came upon her gradually? She faced some legitimate difficulties—Lori needed help! But instead of sharing her frustration with her husband and enlisting his help, or perhaps finding a prayer partner to pray with her, she allowed the anger and self-pity to dominate her life. Had she acknowledged the root of anger, repented of it, then asked the Lord for strength to overcome, the anger would not have become entrenched into a stronghold.

Let's examine another woman's struggle against a bondage she found difficult to describe, but which included rejection, low self-esteem, abandonment, depression, and unforgiveness.

RECOVERING STOLEN CHRISTMAS JOY

Doris hated Christmas. For seventeen years she had put on a front, barely making it through the gift-buying and festivities with family or friends. Melancholy moods chased her for six weeks every holiday season. Christmas might mean joy for others. Not for her. Bah, humbug! Finally she recognized the underlying reason: she was in bondage to past memories.

Doris and Don had met in high school, and as soon as she turned nineteen and he twenty-two, they married. From the beginning, she admits, they had two strikes against them: they were very immature, and they didn't know the Lord.

Three Christmases later, ready to split and go their separate ways, they agreed to spend the holidays with her parents without letting them know of their impending divorce. Don was infatuated with a single girl he had met at work, and Doris knew it would be their last Christmas together. As soon as they returned home after the holidays, the marriage was over.

Shortly afterward, Doris became a Christian and realized she needed to forgive her ex-husband for his unfaithfulness and the divorce that followed. As best she knew how, she told God she forgave Don. But seventeen Christmas seasons rolled by, each reminding her of her failed marriage, each full of the same pain and dread.

Then one year just before the holidays, she decided that she wanted to see Don again, who had remarried and now had eight-year-old twins. At about the same time, Doris learned her father was having major surgery. She took a few days' leave to travel to the town where both Don and her father were now living.

"I felt there were unresolved things I wanted to discuss with Don, even after seventeen years," she said. "Christmas was approaching, and those dreaded feelings were cropping up. But I declared to the devil, 'No! You aren't robbing me of any more Christmases.'"

While her father was recuperating, Doris' brother arranged for Don to come and meet her in a corner of the hospital waiting room. There the two talked about issues that had plagued Doris for a long time. She reassured Don of her forgiveness, and he responded by taking the blame for the failure of their marriage. "If we had married five years later, when both of us were more mature, we'd probably still be married today," he told her.

Doris was able to face Don and forgive him, to face the marriage failure and put it behind her once and for all. At last she was able to release the matter into God's hands, then receive his forgiveness for her immature actions at the time she had married. Don's words also blessed and released her. He didn't say she was worthless, or that their break-up was all her fault—only that they had been too young.

Their talk cleared the doubts out of Doris' mind and brought closure to the relationship. Now she could go on with life, her self-esteem intact. Although she realized forgiveness was a major key to breaking her bondage of depression during the holidays, Doris identified additional factors.

"I had been in emotional bondage to him all those years," she told me. "The pain was always there. It was an issue of abandonment. Healing came when I acknowledged it and truly forgave Don for abandoning me. Although I couldn't put that marriage back together, and though it had been a lonely seventeen years, I could now look forward instead of dwelling on the past. I think the key was choosing to forgive, and refusing to allow the devil to rob me of any more holiday seasons."

Just before Christmas, with her father's condition stable, Doris returned to her new job out West. But this holiday season was different. Instead of pain and dread, joy sprang up like a well within her. She went shopping, sang along with the Christmas carols on the radio, and cheerfully put money in the Salvation Army kettles she used to avoid. She genuinely enjoyed Christmas Day with friends from her church. After seventeen years, the emotional bondage finally was broken.

Doris' experience helps us to understand how the enemy takes advantage of hurts, disappointments, and insecurities to keep us in bondage. Let's summarize the steps she took to finally get free:

1. She moved from a state of denial to admitting to herself that she needed to address this problem.

2. She identified her ex-husband as the source of her pain because he had abandoned her.

3. She took action. In her words, "Healing came when I acknowledged it [the emotional bondage] and truly forgave Don for abandoning me." Though she thought she had forgiven him in a general way, she had to address some of the specific events involved. Actually talking to Don in person helped her to do this, and accelerated her healing.

4. Once the issue was settled she put it behind her, determined to look at Christmas with a positive attitude. The enemy no longer is able to steal her joy at Christmastime.

HOW THE ENEMY WORKS

We don't support the extreme idea that every problem you struggle with is caused by a demon, and that expelling the demon expels the problem. That approach is a cop-out. It exempts you from taking responsibility for your own decisions as you grow in Christian maturity. It exempts you from self-discipline.

But scriptural evidence and our experiences in counseling reveal that Satan's schemes or strategies include his attacks against you in your vulnerable areas. Demonic spirits assault your mind and try to draw you into bondage, and to keep you there. The apostle Paul instructs us:

> Be strong in the Lord and in his mighty power. Put on the full armor of God so that you can take your stand against the devil's schemes. For our struggle is not against flesh and blood, but against the rulers, against the authorities, against the powers of this dark world and against the spiritual forces of evil in the heavenly realms. **Ephesians 6:10-12**

Author Tom White says, "Satan uses every means to keep us preoccupied in introspection or stuck in compulsive ruts. We end up enduring lives of quiet defeat, not free to focus on redeeming the unreached."[3]

God does not plan for us to endure lives of "quiet defeat." Yet all of us have areas of weakness which make us vulnerable to the evil one, and which will allow bondages to ensnare us if we resist God's solution.

Some problems, such as child or spousal abuse, are so deep-seated that you may need to seek the aid of a Christian counselor or experienced prayer partner to help you get free. Ask the Lord to lead you to his choice for a counselor or prayer partner. Then, don't become discouraged because freedom may not come quickly. You didn't get into bondage all at once, and getting out may take some time. But if you're moving toward freedom, even though progress seems slow to you, you're headed in the right direction.

God's compassion for us is tender. He is our loving "Abba [literally, *Daddy*] Father" who truly wants his best for his daughters. He longs to free us from these sins and weaknesses, and he wants us to move on with him in joy, unencumbered by chains of bondage.

Yet we do have a responsibility. We don't earn our freedom by good behavior, but we must be willing to throw out the excess baggage that invites bondage. God joins his power with our will to be liberated. Then the freedom he wants us to enjoy is inevitable.

The truths and principles in this book will help you walk free from all kinds of bondages, some of which we'll explore in more detail later on. We don't claim to have all the answers. We simply share from our understanding of Scripture, our own experiences in ministry, and from godly leaders whose wisdom can shed light on the problems. We want to help you to identify the bondages in your life, and provide guidelines to help you walk free.

PRAYER

Lord, I acknowledge that my walk with you is not all that it should be—and I don't want to live a life of defeat. Please help me to identify the bondages in my life and to find the way to freedom. In Jesus' name. Amen.

TWO

God Wants You Free

The Lord is the Spirit who gives them life, and where he is there is freedom. 2 Corinthians 3:17a, LB

God's enemy and ours, Satan, seeks to make women feel inferior, unworthy, and unloved. We've absorbed the idea that to validate our existence—to be accepted and loved by others—we must "perform" at a certain level. So we often strive to be good students, efficient workers, perfect wives, "super moms," and model Christians.

It's as if we set ourselves up to fail. This mind set causes many women to feel they're not "good enough" to deserve God's help in walking free from bondage. Nothing could be further from the truth. The reality of our helpless bondage is the very reason Jesus came to set us free.

BENT IN BONDAGE

Maybe you can identify with the woman in the Bible who had to walk bent over with her face toward the floor. For eighteen long years she had been unable to stand straight or to do much for herself. Yet she faithfully attended synagogue, no doubt lost in the crowd Sabbath after Sabbath. Jesus, noticing her plight, reached out to her with words of life and liberation. "'Woman, you are loosed from your infirmity.' And He laid hands on her, and immediately she was made straight, and glorified God" (Lk 13:12b-13, NKJV). In essence he was saying, "Woman, you are free! Lift up your head! No more bondage!"

Can you imagine what it must have felt like to stand up straight for the first time in eighteen years? To be able to look into Jesus' eyes of love and compassion and realize, "He really cares about me!" Surely the joy of the Lord engulfed her as she began to praise and glorify God.

When rulers of the synagogue were indignant because Jesus healed on the Sabbath, Jesus asked, "Ought not this woman, being a daughter of Abraham, whom Satan has bound these eighteen years, be loosed from this bond on the Sabbath?" (Lk 13:16, NKJV).

The obvious answer is, Of course she should!

This nameless woman is much like the women we've talked to in our travels all over the world. We meet them in church groups, Bible schools, prayer lines, women's retreats, and on airplanes. Not all are physically bound and crippled as this woman was, but many are spiritually and emotionally bound. And many have been in church for years, yet have never found the complete freedom for which they yearn.

LOOSED, UNTIED

Jesus wants you—and the countless women we have met—set free from every bondage, just as he wanted the "daughter of Abraham" to be loosed. The Greek word for loose in that passage means "to loose anything tied or fastened; to set free; to discharge from prison. Also to free from bondage or disease (one held by Satan) by restoration to health."[1]

His desire to liberate us caused Jesus to come to earth in human form and make the supreme sacrifice to gain our freedom: "Since the children [that means us] have flesh and blood, he too shared in their humanity so that by his death he [Jesus] might destroy him who holds the power of death—that is, the devil—and free those who all their lives were held in slavery by their fear of death" (Heb 2:14-15).

Because he walked this earth just like you and me, Jesus can empathize with the pain of our bondages. But because of his purity and holiness, his victory over sin and Satan makes our release from bondage possible.

Perhaps you feel your situation is hopeless—that your bondage is too entrenched for you ever to experience freedom. You can replace your despair with hope. Let's look at another biblical story about an unnamed woman who was touched and changed by Jesus.

RESCUED AT THE WELL

This woman of Samaria had been married five times, and in her quest for love was now living with a man who was not her husband. Going alone to the well at midday, she probably hoped to avoid the scornful looks of the other women of the village (Jn 4:1-41).

But there she met a stranger who did not scorn her. It was Jesus, who simply asked, "Will you give me a drink?" Not only was he talking to a woman—something a Jewish religious teacher didn't ordinarily do—but to a Samaritan, an ethnic group traditionally hated by the Jews. Throughout the story, Jesus' words and actions demonstrate that women are greatly valued in the kingdom of God. Of course that's why Satan is bent on hindering their ability to be free in Christ.

Jesus knew from the beginning that the woman at the well was "a sinner woman." Yet he pulled her from her despair, offered her the living water of eternal life, and told her—a most unlikely audience for such amazing news—that he was the Messiah. He did not condemn her for her sinful life. He simply offered her the antidote for sin and bondage.

Transformed by her encounter with this man who treated her with dignity and offered her hope, she rushed unashamedly to urge the villagers to come meet Jesus. They, too, were changed because of her testimony and Jesus' teaching.

You can also be transformed, released from bondage. Jesus does not condemn you because you've been ensnared by the enemy. Rather, he provides the solution. Scripture declares: "Whenever anyone turns to the Lord from his sins, then the veil is taken away. The Lord is the Spirit who gives them life, and where he is there is freedom.... We Christians have no veil over our faces; we can be mirrors that brightly reflect the glory of the Lord. And as the Spirit of the Lord works within us, we become more and more like him" (2 Cor 3:16-18, LB).

OVERCOMING THE BONDS OF CHILDHOOD

Perhaps you can identify with Linda's story because of similar bondages in your own life or in the life of someone you know.

Linda had gone to church and Christian schools all her life, yet she said, "I'd never been told that Christians have authority over Satan and his demons. I had believed the lie 'There's nothing you can do.'"

She had a troubled childhood with a manic-depressive mother and a withdrawn, passive father. Her mother sometimes ignored Linda and her siblings altogether; other times she demanded perfection and punished severely for any slight mistake.

"As we grew older the physical abuse stopped, but the mind games became worse as her illness progressed until she became totally psychotic. My search for love and acceptance led to a life of promiscuity. Ken and I got married when I was eighteen because I was pregnant, then the baby was stillborn—not a good beginning for a marriage."

Over the next few years Linda gave birth to two daughters while Ken went from one low-paying job to another. She blamed him for their financial problems, and her unhappiness plunged her into a deep depression.

"In my state of depression I started having nightmares and memory flashes of the childhood abuse—yet I didn't know what to do about it. Soon Ken lost his job and we had to move back to the town I grew up in—which meant facing the 'demons' of my past."

But since Linda had no knowledge of Scripture or inner strength for dealing with these pressures, she dealt with them the way many people do: instead of turning to God, she turned to food.

"Eventually I weighed 200 pounds, had a continually messy home, and a terrible sex life with my husband," she said. "Then one day I found a set of pornographic books Ken had hidden under the towels in the bathroom cupboard—I had never seen anything so perverted. I confronted him immediately, and he seemed truly repentant at the time. I felt betrayed, used, angry, ugly, and fat. The marriage I thought was basically OK was a lie like everything else. How could I survive?"

FREE AT LAST

When it seemed despair would engulf her, Jesus reached out to Linda just as he had done for the Samaritan woman at the well.

"My finding Ken's porn books had brought on this crisis," she reported, "but the turning point came with a second set of books. I began attending a ladies' class that was studying a book on spiritual warfare, and I read some other material on the subject. As I renewed my relationship with God and learned about taking a stand against the enemy, I began breaking the bondages in the name of Jesus. He enabled me to forgive my parents and others who had wounded me, and showed me I could walk in freedom.

"The addiction to food, the promiscuity, living as a victim

er than a victor, the depression, the perfectionism, the anger and resentment—I'm not bound by any of these things anymore. When I repented, then renounced the spirits behind this behavior, I began to get the upper hand in my struggle against depression and all that came with it. I found the Scriptures that tell me who I really am in Christ, and I have laid claim to those.

"All the negative circumstances in my life have not changed. But, Oh, how God has changed me! Because I'm no longer in bondage to food, I've lost forty pounds over the past few months. God has powerfully and mightily done what I tried in vain to do for years—he is helping me to control my appetite and my cravings.

"Now my marriage really is OK. God opened my eyes to Ken's bondage to pornography, but he also showed me how to forgive him and why it had happened. I had not been obedient to the instructions given in 1 Corinthians 7:3-5a:

> The husband should fulfill his marital duty to his wife, and likewise the wife to her husband. The wife's body does not belong to her alone but also to her husband. In the same way, the husband's body does not belong to him alone but also to his wife. Do not deprive each other except by mutual consent and for a time, so that you may devote yourselves to prayer.

"For several months now I have been able to respond freely to Ken's sexual advances, which has helped to heal both of us," she wrote.

Linda discovered she had to withstand the enemy to keep her victory, and she's learned how to use her spiritual weapons to cope with life. But she realizes there are no "once-and-for-all" solutions to her problems. God always wants us to participate with him in our progressive walk to freedom.

"I still have a battle with food, but I am no longer bound by a craving for it," she explains. "I have to choose not to eat outside of stomach hunger. Old habits do die hard, but I know that if I persevere, God will help me overcome that unnatural desire. I can tell a difference on the days when I pray, praise, and read the Word—and the days I don't.

"Now Ken has gotten a good job, and he was promoted to a supervisor's position. At last he is able to use his college training and he has regular hours, which makes life more stable for the family. We have begun to tithe, and God is opening Ken's eyes to the blessings of serving the Lord. He's seen all the changes in me, and he's really starting to believe that God can take care of our every need!"

Notice that her victory is retained when she prays, praises, and reads the Word. Only in God's strength can we hope to stay free. Linda admits old habits die hard and some days can be more struggle-free than others.

GOD'S FREE GIFT

Author Max Lucado discusses our reluctance to answer God's call to freedom:

> We take our free gift and try to earn it or diagnose it or pay for it instead of simply saying "thank you" and accepting it. Ironic as it may appear, one of the hardest things to do is to be saved by grace. There's something in us that reacts to God's free gift. We have some weird compulsion to create laws, systems, and regulations that will make us "worthy" of our gift. Why do we do that? The only reason I can figure is pride. To accept grace means to accept its necessity, and most folks don't like to do that. To accept grace also means that one realizes his despair, and most people aren't too keen on doing that either.... Why some prefer to stay in prison while the cell door has been unlocked is a mystery worth pondering.[2]

Remember, women, we are greatly valued in the kingdom of God! Right now you may have allowed a hidden bondage to hinder your walk with the Lord and rob you of much of what God has for you. But you need not stay in that condition. Whatever your pain or weakness, God's power can overcome the bondage.

Maybe it's been ages since you realized who you are and who you belong to. If Jesus is your Lord, you are a cherished daughter of the King! Begin your steps out of bondage by affirming what God's Word says about you, and refuse to identify with the enemy's accusations against you. Agreeing with the Word of God is one sure way to victory—over insecurity, low self-esteem, inferiority, anger, lust—or whatever captivity you find yourself in right now.

AGREEING WITH GOD

Now that you are ready to get out of bondage, a good starting place is to renew your mind with the Scriptures, reassuring yourself as to who you are in the Lord and what he wants for you. Why not personalize some of these verses, saying them aloud. Here are some good starters:

> "For I know the plans I have for you," declares the Lord, "plans to prosper you and not to harm you, plans to give you hope and a future." **Jeremiah 29:11**

> With us is the Lord our God to help us and to fight our battles. **2 Chronicles 32:8b**

> God is at work in [me] to will and to work for *His* good pleasure. **Philippians 2:13, NASB**

> Forgetting what *lies* behind and reaching forward to what *lies* ahead, I press on toward the goal for the prize of the upward call of God in Christ Jesus. **Philippians 3:13b-14, NASB**

He restores my soul. He guides me in paths of righteousness for his name's sake.

Psalm 23:3

Do not gloat over me, my enemy! Though I have fallen, I will rise.

Micah 7:8a

The Lord is my strength and my shield; my heart trusts in him, and I am helped. My heart leaps for joy and I will give thanks to him in song.

Psalm 28:7

PRAYER FOR FREEDOM

Thank you, Lord, for providing the way for me to walk free from bondage. I acknowledge that I can't do this by myself. I renounce my pride and ask for your help.

Lord, show me the dark corners of my heart that I need to open up to your light. Give me the courage to allow your grace to heal and restore those areas I've tried to keep hidden. Help me to cooperate with the Holy Spirit; strengthen me to stand against the enemy. I choose to obey you and to walk away from every bondage in my life. Thank you for setting me free, in Jesus' name. Amen.

THREE

The Bondage of Grief and Disappointment

> *...a man of sorrows, and acquainted with grief.... He [Christ] has borne our griefs and carried our sorrows.*
> **Isaiah 53:3b, 4**

Grief—that heart-stabbing emotion that almost takes your breath away—is a slice of life we all experience eventually. It comes with varying intensity. But as a part of our sinful heritage its coming is certain. The question is, how will we respond to it?

I (Ruthanne) remember hearing the story of a family who bought a new home and redecorated it to suit their tastes exactly. But before moving from their farmhouse into the new house in town, their teenage daughter and only child was killed in an accident. The grief-stricken mother refused to move into the new house, claiming her daughter's spirit may someday return to the house where she'd grown up. The girl's bedroom remained just as she had left it on the day of her death. The new house, with drapes closed, stood empty year after year.

This is a picture of a woman literally "stuck" in the pain and denial of her loss because she would not permit her grief to follow its natural course to resolution.

We tend to think of grief in relation to the death of a loved one—obviously a major source of grief. But this powerful emotion also may come crashing into your life when you experience:

- divorce
- a broken friendship or relationship
- loss of a job
- loss of personal property
- loss of independence
- loss of an opportunity you had counted on
- disappointment with yourself
- disappointment with a loved one (especially a child)
- failure to achieve a goal

Life contains many losses and disappointments which bring grief to our door, but this visitor actually can be good when seen in perspective. Grief serves as an escape valve for our emotions like a tea kettle's valve which allows steam to escape. It helps us acknowledge the loss, resolve the pain, then move forward. But grief becomes a bondage for those who don't find God's help in seeking release.

A JAB OF MEMORY

Perhaps you will identify with journal entries written by well-known author C.S. Lewis when he lost his wife to cancer after only two years of marriage:

> No one ever told me that grief felt so like fear. I am not afraid, but the sensation is like being afraid. The same fluttering in the stomach, the same restlessness, the yawning. I keep on swallowing.
>
> ... There are moments, most unexpectedly, when something inside me tries to assure me that I don't really mind so much, not so very much, after all. Love is not the whole of a man's

life.... I've plenty of what are called "resources."... Come, I shan't do so badly. One is ashamed to listen to this voice but it seems for a little to be making out a good case. Then comes a sudden jab of red-hot memory and all this "commonsense" vanishes like an ant in the mouth of a furnace.[1]

THE GRIEF OF DISAPPOINTMENT

Disappointments such as the following ones which women have shared with us can imprison you if you don't yield them to the Lord.

- A young woman's fiancé backs out of marriage six weeks before the wedding.
- A barren wife longs to have a baby of her own.
- A mother discovers her daughter is in a lesbian relationship.
- A woman learns her colleague got the promotion she was hoping for.
- A young wife struggles because her husband can't hold a job and adequately provide for the family.
- A mother who's worked to provide an education for her son is told he has no intention of going to college.

Whether your grief stems from a divorce, the death of a loved one, a broken relationship, or some other disappointment, it's important that you not get "stuck" in this grief through denial, depression, or blaming. Don't allow the rest of your life to be defined by the loss you've suffered.

The enemy will do everything he can to prey on your grief and keep you bound to it. But we Christians need not grieve without hope, as unbelievers do (see 1 Thessalonians 4:13). In our trial of grief we still have hope, because we have access to the promises of God and his comfort. Paul reminds us of this:

> What a wonderful God we have—he is the Father of our Lord Jesus Christ, the source of every mercy, and the one who so wonderfully comforts and strengthens us in our hardships and trials. And why does he do this? So that when others are troubled, needing our sympathy and encouragement, we can pass on to them this same help and comfort God has given us.
>
> **2 Corinthians 1:3-4, LB**

The principles we suggest in this chapter will help you go through a healthy grieving process.

GRIEF HEALING

Different personality types respond to grief in different ways, but counselors and therapists generally agree that grieving is a process which may take up to two years to complete.

Anyone who has suffered a traumatic loss, then gone through the stages of grieving, will agree that it is work—requiring spiritual, emotional, and physical energy. Some women feel overwhelmed by the effort involved and seek to avoid it. But avoidance doesn't substitute for grieving—it only postpones it. And the repressed, unprocessed grief leads to bondage.

We could look at this process as being four tasks of grief:

1. The primary task is acceptance—simply facing the reality that you have suffered the loss. The greater the loss, the more difficult this task will be.
2. To feel the pain—our aversion to pain causes us to want to avoid this step. Some people medicate their pain with alcohol or drugs, or numb it through work, socializing, busyness, travel, etc. But sooner or later, whether correctly or incorrectly, we must experience the pain.
3. To adjust to an environment in which the deceased (or the job, relationship, goal, etc.) is missing. To do this, mourners must

believe in themselves, learn new skills, and take on new responsibilities. Widows who already lack self-confidence and who have few job skills find difficulty with this. The joy of the Lord truly has to be their strength.

4. To withdraw emotional energy and reinvest in another relationship. Sometimes people find it easier to hold on to the dead than to take the necessary risks involved in reinvesting in the living. This is the reorganization phase of the grief process.

COPING WITH MULTIPLE LOSSES

Let's examine how one woman, experiencing multiple losses over a few short years, illustrates this process.

Maidee lost her older son in a car wreck, her husband to divorce, and her mother to Alzheimer's disease. How did she handle such overwhelming grief—her son's life cut short, her husband's desertion after twenty-seven years of marriage, and the pain of seeing her mother become so confused that she barely knew her own daughter?

The tragedy of her son's death was compounded by Maidee's realization that her husband was slipping away—lured by forces that she does not yet fully understand. "These forces were attracted to Joe, or Joe to them, like nails to a magnet," she shared. "And when he had slipped too far for me to reach, Psalm 37 became my secret security. As the real Joe disappeared, I hid myself under that psalm until it surrounded me like a blanket. 'Fret not thyself because of evildoers....'" (KJV).

The evildoers brazenly swept into Maidee's life like a flood by way of hang-up phone calls, threatening messages, wild car chases. She had her phone tapped because of tormenting calls she received—from her husband's wild friends, she suspected.

"He frequently wanted me to go partying with them," she related, "but I just couldn't. Joe was living two lives—one as an upright businessman who was a regular church attender, and the other as a very suspicious character, perhaps as a drug dealer—I never knew for sure. He would put his arm around me in church on Sundays—the perfect Christian husband. But at home when we were alone he shouted vile obscenities at me, and finally moved out of our bedroom.

"Whenever our younger son came home from college, Joe would behave like Mr. Good Guy. But on ordinary days, he'd go out to his workshop in the backyard, turn on the radio, and then disappear for hours at a time with no explanation.

"Joe never wanted me to work—though I had teaching credentials—and I later learned he had quietly spread around the lie that I had suffered a nervous breakdown. I could have felt like a victim in this situation, but I was saturated in Psalm 37, especially verse 12: 'The wicked plot against the righteous and gnash their teeth at them; but the Lord laughs at the wicked, for he knows their day is coming.'

"The Lord gave me the wisdom to not allow Joe to suddenly put our house in his name only. He also led me to vary my schedule and driving routes to evade the mysterious people who often tried to follow me—Joe's unsavory companions, I suspected. Perhaps their intent was to threaten me in trying to collect old debts from Joe. As I sensed the Lord laughing at the meanness surrounding me, I was able to stay joyful and hopeful. And during this time my younger son fell in love with the Lord as a bonus."

One night Maidee told Joe that she felt he likely had been exposed to the AIDS virus because of the company he'd been keeping. He reacted with shock, as he thought he'd kept her from finding out who his companions were. "After that he grew very uncomfortable being around me, and within a short time he filed for a no-fault divorce and left town," Maidee reported. "I was delivered from the bondage of a bad marriage to a devious man who screamed insults at me. I was also now free from shadowy threats and unnamed dangers, and always having to check to see if someone was following me."

Maidee did not believe in divorce; one had never occurred in her family. But here she was, divorced. Yet free. And safe. For a while, Maidee went to live with her mother.

"Mom was my best friend in the world, my always-ally," Maidee said. "But when I ran home, I ran home to Alzheimer's. As Mom's condition deteriorated, her winsome personality turned dark and scary. Her health changed from robust to fragile. Then came the years of confusion, fury, and dementia.

"Yet with all of that came a wonderful gift for me from the Lord. It seemed he always came in mighty force to meet my need, or sent someone. When Mom died it was a blessed relief for her. I was physically tired to the marrow, mentally and emotionally depleted. But the new gift continued for me. Passages of Scripture—Psalm 42, for example—leaped off the page into my heart.

"In and out of dark nights, dreary mornings, and empty afternoons—from the radio, the television, a random page in a brand-new book, came someone either proclaiming or explaining Psalm 42:1: 'As the deer panteth for the water, so my soul longeth after Thee....'

"I sold my portion of the house and moved away to start my life all over again. Now I'm living in a tiny town in a tiny cottage, but the Lord has surrounded me with his peace, his love, and his favor. Although I'm sometimes lonesome, this life of peace is much better than the bondage I was in when I feared for my very life and put up with being called every foul name in the book."

Maidee is a healthy example of a resilient woman who, despite appalling tragedies, met the grieving process head-on and walked through it. She says that for her the steps through grief which kept her out of bondage were:

1. Focusing on the Lord and believing his special promises for me—especially his protection. Depending on him as my source of strength.
2. Asking his guidance and discernment before making any decisions—having the phone tapped, when and where I drove my car, who not to talk with, etc.

3. Moving away to start life over—leaving behind a large comfortable house and my church friends. This change of scenery was critical for me.
4. Guarding myself from bitterness, assured that the Lord would fight my battles for me.

"Why all the battles? I don't know. But I do know that God is good. He is always victorious, and nothing is ever wasted in the life of a child of his. Everything that happens to a child of God will all fit together some way, someday, into something very beautiful and extremely valuable."

There may be times, even in the natural process of grieving, when memories will evoke deeply hidden emotions. But they needn't drag you into bondage.

TEARS OF PAIN

After Karen lost her mother, waves of grief would engulf her at the most unexpected times. One day she went into a bakery to buy blueberry muffins for an office party. At the counter, tears unexpectedly sprang from her eyes and her hands began trembling. In her mind's eye she saw a picture of her mom in the kitchen baking her favorite—blueberry muffins. Leaving the muffins on the counter, Karen ran from the store, got into her car, and drove until she gained control of her emotions and her tears. Then she went into another bakery and bought muffins for the party.

"It took me a little over a year to work through the memories and accept losing Mom," she said. "But now I can encourage others—go ahead and cry when you feel like it. Just remember the Lord of comfort is there for you. He will never leave you or forsake you."

Karen's experience, though painful, illustrates the process of healthy grief—allowing herself to feel the pain and express it, then move toward resolution. Today, buying blueberry muffins brings nostalgic memories, but her pain has healed.

TEARS OF HEALING

Once after I (Ruthanne) spoke at a retreat in New York, a young mother—we'll call her Laura—came to me for prayer and counsel. "I don't understand why my anger has begun to get out of control the last several months," she said. "I find myself overreacting when my four-year-old daughter misbehaves. I spank her too hard. Sometimes I get angry and yell at her for no real reason. I've prayed about it, and my husband has prayed with me, but it keeps happening. It frightens me...."

I began to pray, asking the Lord to give revelation and insight about her problem. Shortly I felt impressed to ask her a few questions about her family background and her experience with the Lord. Laura shared with me that her father had died when she was four years old. Her mother and other well-meaning relatives felt she was too young to go to the funeral, so they shielded her from all the events surrounding the death. They offered no explanations about what had happened, and at age four she was too bewildered to ask meaningful questions or fathom the tragedy. She only knew that her daddy never came home again.

In the years that followed, Laura's unresolved grief became a deep-seated anger toward God for depriving her of a father during her growing-up years. She learned more about the facts of his death, but she never worked through the emotional impact of the event. Her repressed feelings, though she was not consciously aware of them, didn't go away. When her own little girl reached age four (the age she had been when her father died) anger began cropping up again—primarily toward her daughter, but also toward her husband and sometimes toward herself.

"Laura, I feel the key to this issue is that you were never permitted to mourn your father's death," I said. "Your family felt they were protecting you from the impact of your loss. Though they meant well, that only repressed the grief and kept you from expressing your feelings. It's OK to feel the pain of that disappointment, and even to feel angry—that's a normal human response. It was not God's will for you to be fatherless, but in our fallen world these things happen. Let's ask the Lord to help you release your anger and express your feelings about losing your dad."

I took Laura's hand and began praying for God to reveal his father-love to her, and to help her understand he did not inflict this tragedy upon her. I asked him to comfort the little girl who had lost her daddy. As I prayed Laura began to weep. I put my arms around her and comforted her as if she were four years old. For several minutes she sobbed like a child as I held her and reassured her, "It's OK to cry, Laura. Now talk to God—tell him how you feel—express your grief and disappointment."

She sobbed as she poured her heart out to God, but when her tears subsided she looked up with a new brightness in her eyes. "I guess I really was angry about not having a father while growing up, and not understanding it. But my heart feels different now, and I think things will be different when I go back home."

I counseled Laura to continue talking to the Lord about her father's death, holding nothing back and allowing him to continue her healing. She left the retreat feeling she had been freed from a bondage she couldn't even identify.

Joanne Smith, author of *How to Say Goodbye*, says there are healthy and unhealthy tears. She writes:

> There is a point in the crying process when the physical and emotional release has taken place, but we fail to move it to a point of hope. At the end of a crying session, we should feel better, not hopeless.... Remember, grief is painful, but you decide if it will crush you or create new life in you.
>
> Tears are beneficial as long as we learn to release them in a way that draws us to our God of hope. This is not meant to be a super-spiritual pat answer, but a workable truth.... When fear picks up where the tears left off, we've made a wrong turn.[2]

HUMOR HELPS

Author and humorist Barbara Johnson has helped many people on their journey of grief by getting them to laugh. Despite the death of one son in Vietnam, another in a car crash, and years of being alienated from a third son because of his homosexual lifestyle, Barbara exudes joy because she's learned to laugh in spite of life's tragedies. She writes:

> Humor helps to combat my own grief and helps me accelerate the grief process for others. I love little quips and quotes and have collected hundreds of them over the years. Humor is not something to be used to make fun of a situation, only to make fun out of what seems to be a hopeless catastrophe. Folks need something that will help get them through the times when nothing seems to calm them, not even reminders of comfort from the Bible given by well-meaning Christian friends. It's not that these scriptures aren't true; it's just that the pain is so intense you can't appreciate what the words are saying right at that moment. Later these scripture verses can become very meaningful, but, ironically, there were times during my own sieges of grief that the following observation made a kind of crazy sense to me: "Man cannot live by bread alone; he needs peanut butter, too."[3]

We can learn from Barbara not to take ourselves too seriously, and to indulge in laughter from time to time. It helps prevent your becoming locked into grief. Disappointment and grief, while unpleasant, can provide seasons of spiritual growth and intimacy with your heavenly Father.

Remember, the only healthy solution to grief is to surrender it to God. You can begin now by praying the following prayer and giving your hurt to him. Burying your grief or disappointment, or masking it with addictions, does not cure it. It only becomes a deep bondage of anger and resentment—a problem we examine in the next chapter.

PRAYER

Lord, so often I feel I can't cope with my grief and disappointments. You were a man of sorrows, so I know you can understand my hurt. Help me to cast my disappointments and grief on you, and receive your comfort. Thank you for caring for me, Lord. Please begin the healing process in my heart. And while I still feel so vulnerable, please remind others to pray for me until I reach complete recovery. Lord, restore my soul, especially my emotions. Thank you, precious Savior. Amen.

FOUR

Anger That Imprisons

If you are angry, don't sin by nursing your grudge. Don't let the sun go down with you still angry—get over it quickly; for when you are angry you give a mighty foothold to the devil. **Ephesians 4:26-27, LB**

Anger! We women often have difficulty with this powerful emotion because from childhood we've acquired the idea that it's not "ladylike" to express anger. When we do give vent to expressing our anger, we often feel guilty afterward because we believe getting angry is sinful.

Like grief, anger can be good. Emotions are God-given, and expressing our emotions in healthy ways is God's plan for us. But women often feel victimized by the strength of their emotions, or the fear of them. These fears lead us to deny, repress, over-express, or manipulate our emotions, instead of dealing with them head-on. Anger is perhaps hardest to handle, especially if we've stored it up only to overreact to a relatively minor infraction.

Scripture does not forbid anger. It teaches that:

1. When you do become angry, do not sin.
2. Do not go to bed at night while still angry.

Why is this so important? Because stored-up anger becomes corrosive and dangerous. It's like putting a tempest in a teapot; if not calmed, it's bound to cause destruction.

LOSS AND VICTIMIZATION

Anger almost always begins with a perceived loss, an actual loss, or the threat of a loss. The loss itself, coupled with the feeling that you're being victimized, produces anger. These are some of the losses we suffer in life which may provoke anger:

- Loss of control—such as being required to abide by rules with which we don't agree and which hamper freedoms we believe to be personal rights.
- Losing effectiveness in influencing the behavior of our children, or of another close family member or friend.
- Loss of valued relationships—through death, infidelity, divorce, misunderstanding, hurt feelings, relocation.
- Loss of valued role—through retirement, layoff, dismissal, reassignment, etc.
- Loss of valued possessions—through carelessness, theft, floods, fires, storms, repossession of property.
- Loss of skills or abilities—through accidents, war injuries, debilitating illnesses, senility.
- Loss of self-esteem—when we think we've failed or not lived up to our own standards or those of others.
- Loss of face—public exposure of one's failures or inadequacies; humiliation; false accusations of wrong-doing.
- Loss of virginity—due to illicit sex, rape, or abuse.
- Loss of childhood—due to abandonment, abuse, lack of nurturing, poverty, etc.

- Threat of physical harm or violence.
- Threat of assault on one's character or reputation.

Generally, we feel strong anger when we feel our expectations and perceived personal rights have been violated—the right to personal safety and a peaceful life, the right to having our possessions inviolate, a right to privacy, or a right to have and express an opinion.

In a marriage, both the husband and the wife expect certain things of the relationship—some of them conscious, many of them unconscious. Often "his list" and "her list" contrast sharply, with only a few items overlapping. For example, the wife may feel she has a "right" to have her husband converse with her and exchange experiences and ideas when he comes home from work. He may feel he has a "right" to some peace and quiet after a stressful day at the office. If neither of them is aware of the other's expectations or "list of rights," conflict is inevitable. But, if both parties clearly and honestly express these feelings and clarify their expectations, instead of seething because "my husband (wife) doesn't understand me," the resolved conflict produces a stronger relationship.

If pressed to put into words exactly what we do expect from a relationship, we may feel embarrassed to realize our goals seem selfish or childish. However, the more unexpressed expectations or rights we lay claim to, the more numerous our opportunities to become angry.

IS ALL ANGER SINFUL?

Anger of itself is not sinful; it is the wrong expression of anger which is sinful. Jesus himself became angry when he drove the money-changers out of the temple and when the scribes and Pharisees objected because he healed a man on the Sabbath Day (see John 2:13-17 and Mark 3:1-5).

Commentator William Barclay writes:

> There were times when Jesus was terribly and majestically angry.... The anger which is selfish and uncontrolled is a sinful and hurtful thing, which must be banished from the Christian life. But the selfless anger which is disciplined into the service of Christ and of our fellow men is one of the great dynamic forces of the world.[1]

An example that illustrates Barclay's point is the founding of MADD (Mothers Against Drunk Driving). This group of women, many of whom have had the grief of losing a child in a drunk-driving accident, lobby for legislation to keep convicted offenders off the roadways. Their anger over the needless death of a loved one is channeled toward helping save the lives of others.

We tend to think of anger as a negative emotion, but it also has a positive side. In times of danger anger helps activate our instinct for self-preservation, and causes physiological responses such as increased flow of adrenaline, escalation of blood pressure and pulse, increased perspiration, rapid breathing, and tensed muscles. This "fight or flight" mode prepares us to respond to danger, but it also may cause headaches, nausea, stomachaches, or other maladies if the anger is not expressed appropriately. Psychologically, feeling that we are powerless victims, discounted, or ignored, causes anger and a desire for revenge.

Many psychologists believe that anger can be eradicated more easily once we have allowed ourselves to admit it and to feel it. Abuse counselors agree that victims need to express their anger to "get it out of their system"—then they can move toward healing. If we deny our anger, it remains hidden, waiting to be felt.

In other words, if we express anger in appropriate ways, we get rid of it. But if we repress it, or force it underground, it leads to bondage.

RESENTMENT PREVENTS LOVE

One mother's painful experience illustrates this principle. Roberta couldn't stand her adopted son, Sam, but she didn't know why. She and her husband had adopted a baby girl eighteen months before getting Sam, and Roberta adored her.

After adopting their first daughter, she and her husband had applied to adopt a second girl. But months later, when they were called to the hospital to see a baby available for adoption, they discovered the infant was a boy.

"I guess we'll take him, because I want us to have two children," she told her husband. But once they brought the baby home, she discovered that she was unable to form the same bond with this baby that she had experienced with her first adopted child. Whenever he cried at night, Roberta would get up and feed him, but she just couldn't love him.

Within the next three years she had two daughters of her own—both of them unexpected miracles. She had no problems loving them and bonding with them. But there was something about Sam she couldn't stand. Throughout his years in school, Sam's teachers frequently called Roberta to come to the school. He seemed bent on disrupting every class, acting up to get attention.

"I developed a hatred toward him," she said. "But at the same time, I hated myself for the way I treated him. He never seemed to do anything to please me. It was obvious that for him, negative attention was better than no attention at all. Others saw me as being a great Christian mother, but inside I felt horribly guilty."

Year after year Roberta fought her feelings of anger toward her son. The slightest infraction made her furious, and she would punish him more severely than his sisters. One day she went on a crying jag over Sam and ended up in the hospital for two weeks of rest. But that didn't help matters. The bondage of hate and guilt remained, and was about to devour her.

She dreaded Sam's coming home from school in the afternoons—all she wanted was for him to stay out of her sight. When he got in trouble during his high school years, she would take his car keys and ground him. But in a few days she gave the keys back just to keep from having to drive him to school.

All this time Roberta and her husband attended church, where she had received the baptism of the Holy Spirit. Then one day in Bible study, a verse jumped out at her: "Anyone who claims to be in the light but hates his brother is still in the darkness.... Anyone who hates his brother is a murderer, and you know that no murderer has eternal life in him" (1 Jn 2:9; 3:15).

The more Scriptures Roberta read, the more she realized she was really a murderer in her heart. She began to pray, "Holy Spirit, free my spirit to be able to forgive and love this boy."

In church a few Sundays later the pastor said, "Ask the Holy Spirit what he wants you to do today." Roberta practically ran to the front of the sanctuary to confess her need to be free of the hatred and years of accumulated anger. She admitted to those who gathered around her to pray that she felt great hatred toward her son, even though he was now twenty-one years old and married. As she repented and cried tears of remorse and regret, she received the Lord's forgiveness.

Then she remembered that when she had been sixteen, her own mother had given birth to a baby boy. Roberta thought he was simply wonderful—that there could never be another little boy like him. When Sam didn't measure up to her idealized memory of her baby brother, she repressed her disappointment and anger and tried to make the best of it. But it took its toll.

Roberta had been totally unaware of this buried anger until she prayed to have hate replaced with God's love—the love that's poured out in our hearts by the Holy Spirit (see Romans 5:5).

"All the blackness in me—that tar—was replaced by Jesus' light," she reported. "God began to give me love for my son—the same as I had for my girls. It was glorious!"

God had answered her prayer, but she also knew she had to confess her sin and to ask for her son's forgiveness. The next day Roberta sat down with her son and asked him to forgive her. He later sent her a Mother's Day card saying she was the best mother any son could ever have. Now she has a loving relationship with Sam and his wife and children.

ANGER AND DEPRESSION

Women tend to see themselves in the role of peacemakers and nurturers, and thus feel they must always place their own needs last, which sometimes leads to repressed anger and resentment. But when anger is repressed it often shows up in the form of depression. This is precisely the inner conflict Roberta was dealing with. Counselor and author Dr. H. Norman Wright shares this insight:

> It is not feminine to be angry. Thus, many women are stuck with their anger and have nowhere to take it. And many learn to experience hurt rather than becoming angry in certain situations. The anger builds up over the years and when it is released it carries with it the accumulated residue. The result is overreaction.... When expressing anger, many women also express tears, guilt or sorrow. But this contaminates the expression of anger and confuses those around them. Many women quickly shift their feelings of anger into hurt. It is safer.
>
> ... Many men and women experience depression when they bottle up their anger. In fact, repressed anger is one of the major causes of depression. It is a dangerous way to handle anger because the anger remains alive inside us, churning around and looking for a way to come out. For many women, this is a learned response because of a lack of encouragement to experience anger.[2]

ANGER STEALS JOY

What happens when anger is not properly expressed or channeled? It doesn't go away. It is "displaced," or directed toward persons other than the one who caused the anger—sometimes directed toward oneself and exhibited in self-destructive behavior. Many suicides are likely in this category. Or the anger is "internalized," and may cause physical maladies or social and relationship problems.

Jolene is a woman whose repressed anger toward her parents has almost completely deprived her of any joy in life. And it causes her to look almost seventy years old, instead of fifty. She and her brother were reared in an ultra-legalistic religious home where expressions of love, tenderness, or encouragement were nonexistent. In her early childhood Old Testament Bible stories were read to her at bedtime, followed by the admonition, "You'd better be good, or God will get you!" Then her father or mother would turn out the light, slam the door, and leave her in the darkened room shivering with fright.

She remembers hearing her brother scream as her father beat him, and running from the house to escape the sounds. Her parents figuratively "beat her up" with the Word of God, berating her for not living up to their interpretation of its standards. Not once did her parents say, "I love you," or tell her that Jesus died on the cross because he loved her. Only that she would be judged for her sins, which they constantly pointed out to her.

This distorted view of God caused Jolene to be angry with him, but she couldn't bring herself to admit it. She assumed, "I can never be good enough to please God, no matter how I try. Since I'm doomed to hell anyway, I may as well live life just as I please."

In reflecting on her childhood she said to a counselor, "I should have loved my parents, but I was afraid of them. I could never please them, yet felt enormous guilt if I tried to turn my back on them."

All this pent-up anger has led Jolene to become a chain smoker. Nicotene temporarily calms her boiling emotions. She has gone through multiple marriages and is now involved in an adulterous affair—behavior which is highly offensive to her parents. She has taken on a martyr's role where they are concerned. Assuming responsibility for them in their declining years, she visits them frequently to help with shopping, visits to doctors, etc. But it is literally a set-up for more abuse. Displaying neither affection nor gratitude for her help, they continue to belittle her and criticize her lifestyle.

Group therapy and counseling combined could not convince Jolene to acknowledge the source of her anger, forgive her parents, and start down the road toward healing. Her anger and bitterness literally has become her personality. She rebuffed all acts of kindness offered by her therapy group; never once did they see her smile. She acknowledges that she has a problem, which is why she enrolled in group therapy. But she refuses to take responsiblity for her anger.

"Unless Jolene chooses to respond to therapy, I fear her deep anger and rage may literally cause her to suffer an early death," the counselor reported. "I wish I could help her to see that her anger should be directed at the devil for deceiving her parents and keeping them in bondage to a distorted view of the gospel. She could possibly be the key to their freedom."

Jolene is an example of a woman who is in complete bondage to her anger, but who is unwilling to deal with it in order to be free.

GIVING THE DEVIL A FOOTHOLD

How many people do you know who have given the devil a foothold in their lives because they have nursed a grudge or harbored anger and bitterness in their hearts? Are you in this condition yourself? Your anger, not dealt with properly, opens the door to a spirit of anger. As in Jolene's case, it can become a controlling force in your life and keep you in prison.

The way out of this bondage is to follow Paul's advice in Ephesians 4:26-27, the verses we quote at the beginning of the chapter. Get rid of any stored-up anger, and don't allow it to accumulate in the future. With the help of the Holy Spirit you can become like the person spoken of in Proverbs 16:32: "He who is slow to anger is better than the mighty. And he who rules his spirit, than he who captures a city" (NASB).

Dietra is another example of a woman who buried her anger for many years. She grew up in a happy family where her parents never argued nor raised their voices at their two children. But one thing bugged her: her mom waited on her dad hand and foot, even to getting his glasses of water.

As she grew up she was judging her father and unknowingly opened a door to sin. She used to joke, "I think God put me on earth to straighten men out." Throughout her first marriage she battled anger because her husband constantly demeaned her, and the marriage failed.

For ten years she was a single parent, then she met Frank, a dark, handsome businessman. They had a brief courtship, and got married within a few months. It was a good marriage until Dietra began noticing that he was putting her down—and her anger was exploding.

"I was a Christian and had asked the Holy Spirit to guide my life—but in the area of anger I was not yielding to his control," she said. "I could not stand for a man to demean me. At the slightest hint of a put-down—or maybe for no reason at all—I would explode with vile, hateful words.

"I would pray, 'God, somewhere in me I'm still agreeing with this anger and I'm still justifying it. I must get some satisfaction in it or it wouldn't rise up. Lord, I don't hate this sin like you hate it. Make me hate it as you do. Show me how you see it.'"

One day after prayer she realized God wanted her free even more than she did, but she had to cooperate with him. "Lord, I commit my mouth to be used by the Holy Spirit and I will not allow the enemy to use me," she prayed. "I am confessing that in Christ, I have 'a quiet and gentle spirit,' and 'soft answers that turn away wrath.'"

TAMING THE TONGUE

She memorized verses to speak out constantly—verses about the tongue, condition of the heart, anger and wrath. One night at a dinner party when she made an innocent comment that upset her husband, he grabbed her arm and shook her angrily as dinner guests looked on. Though stunned, she didn't retaliate. She was winning her anger battle.

"Because of his Middle Eastern background he was prejudiced against women," she explained. "He values women, but I saw that whenever a woman would disagree with him, a hateful spirit came over him. I was able to separate the person (my husband) from the sin.

"Understanding why he lashed out helped me to realize that every time I responded in the flesh I was working with the enemy. When I cried out to God for help he showed me to stop reacting to my husband's outbursts. But I had to learn how to tap into the Holy Spirit so I would not respond in my natural pattern of anger. Now when he shouts at me, my calm comment might be, 'Oh, lighten up, Frank!'—instead of 'Shut up, you jerk.'"

Dietra said she asked God to forgive her for two key things: for not valuing her husband, and for judging men, including her own father. Her advice to those going through a similar situation: "Don't give in to self-pity; God will strengthen you. Control your thoughts and your words of response. Pray in the Spirit. Memorize pertinent Scriptures. Bind whatever spirits you recognize in the other person—for instance, I bind a haughty spirit in my husband when it operates, but I can't cast it out until he is ready to have it gone. He's started a men's Bible study group and he's confessed his problem to them. Soon he'll be ready to have that bondage broken completely."

If you're facing a bondage like Dietra's, God first wants to deal with you and your own anger—not the other person. At the end of this chapter we've included Scriptures which helped her. You may want to memorize some of them as part of your strategy for victory.

Part of Dietra's struggle in winning her anger battle was learning to allow the Holy Spirit to tame her tongue. It's a problem many women struggle with—not only in regard to anger, but also gossiping, murmuring, and complaining. Scripture speaks strongly concerning this issue:

> But no one can tame the tongue. It is wild and evil. It is full of poison that can kill. We use our tongues to praise our Lord and Father, but then we curse people. And God made them like himself. Praises and curses come from the same mouth! My brothers, this should not happen. **James 3:8-10, NCV**

Pastor David Wilkerson says:

> You can no more tame your tongue by yourself than a wild horse can tame itself. Wild horses are tamed by experienced trainers who "break" them. And the Holy Spirit is our trainer. Only He can break our unruly, wild tongues![3]

SCRIPTURES ON THE TONGUE

> The Lord is compassionate and gracious, slow to anger, abounding in love. **Psalm 103:8**

> He who is slow to anger is better than the mighty, And he who rules his spirit than he who takes a city. **Proverbs 16:32, NKJV**

> ... for out of the overflow of the heart the mouth speaks.
> **Matthew 12:34b**

> In your anger do not sin: Do not let the sun go down while you are still angry, and do not give the devil a foothold.
> **Ephesians 4:26-27**

> Do not let any unwholesome talk come out of your mouths, but only what is helpful for building others up according to their needs, that it may benefit those who listen. And do not

grieve the Holy Spirit of God, with whom you were sealed for the day of redemption. Get rid of all bitterness, rage and anger, brawling and slander, along with every form of malice.

Ephesians 4:29-31

... being confident of this, that he who began a good work in you will carry it on to completion until the day of Christ Jesus.

Philippians 1:6

I can do everything through him who gives me strength.

Philippians 4:13

Put to death, therefore, whatever belongs to your earthly nature.... You used to walk in these ways, in the life you once lived. But now you must rid yourselves of all such things as these: anger, rage, malice, slander, and filthy language from your lips. **Colossians 3:5a, 7-8**

My dear brothers, take note of this: Everyone should be quick to listen, slow to speak and slow to become angry, for man's anger does not bring about the righteous life that God desires.

James 1:19-20

PRAYER TO RELEASE ANGER

Pray this prayer as often as necessary in order to vent your anger and receive God's peace. You also may need to review the steps in forgiving found in chapter thirteen.

Heavenly Father, I admit to you that I am angry; thank you that I can express this to you now. I have been angry with (name) *because* (name the offense). *I feel this is wrong, and I feel violated. But Lord, by an act of my will, I choose to forgive* (name) *for what he (she) has done. Forgive me, Lord, for the thoughts of bitterness, hatred, and* (name your feelings) *that I have allowed to take hold of my life, and for the angry words I have spoken. I release this anger, and I choose to identify with you and your ways. Thank you for the release and the cleansing.*

I pray as King David did, "Set a guard over my mouth, O Lord; keep watch over the door of my lips."[4] Help me to obey you, to walk in love, and to cooperate with the Holy Spirit in controlling my tongue and resolving this conflict. In Jesus' name. Amen.

FIVE

The Bondage of Selfish Ambition

For where you have envy and selfish ambition, there you find disorder and every evil practice. But the wisdom that comes from heaven is first of all pure; then peace-loving, considerate, submissive....

James 3:16-17

"She's a Jezebel—stay away from her!" Ever heard that comment? Probably no woman in the Bible is as despised as Jezebel. Certainly no Christian woman wants to be like her.

Jezebel was the daughter of a priest of Baal who married Ahab, a king of Israel, then caused both him and the nation to turn to worshiping Baal. When a neighbor refused to sell a vineyard her husband wanted to purchase, Jezebel took matters into her own hands and arranged for the man to be falsely accused, then stoned to death (1 Kgs 16:29-33; 21:1-16). We describe her with such unflattering adjectives as seductive, conniving, immoral, devious, manipulative, controlling, treacherous, even murderous.

Obviously she's not a positive role model for women! She personifies the envy and selfish ambition mentioned in the above verse (Jas 3:16). Yet there is within each of us—when we're not completely yielded to the Lord—a tendency to behave like her.

We won't attempt to second-guess why or how Jezebel developed these behavior traits. But through counseling many women over the years, we've found that manipulation and control are fruits which often grow in the soil of insecurity, rejection, and abuse.

Of course, wanting what is right and good does not necessarily classify as "selfish ambition." But problems often develop when we make our own judgments as to what is right and good, then try to make it happen. At the heart of many bondages is willfulness—an unwillingness to surrender to God our wounds, our disappointments, our weaknesses, our fears. Instead we become slaves to all our inclinations.

Why do we manipulate people and circumstances to get what we want? For many, it is behavior learned through parental example. For abuse victims, it often is a defensive measure to protect oneself from being hurt again. In many cases the desired end result is not evil of itself, but our drive to have things our way can trap us in a bondage of willfulness.

WHO'S IN CONTROL?

Over the past twenty years the feminist movement in the United States has fostered the notion that a woman has a right to whatever she wants in order to be happy.

We acknowledge the fact that women in American society, as well as in other cultures, indeed have suffered many types of abuse and discrimination. But as a backlash against what feminists perceive to be suppression of their rights by men, many women have overreacted with deep animosity toward men in general. Some have embraced the philosophy that they can make a life for themselves without a man—including having children without marriage. It's a favorite story line for TV shows. Numerous magazines carry reports of "modern" women who choose to become mothers without being wives.

Consider this *Newsweek* article:

> Especially for women who can afford it, marriage is no longer necessary.... Despite growing recognition by social scientists that children do better in two-parent homes, the number of women going it alone jumped by 60 percent in the last decade, according to U.S. Census Bureau figures released this month. Put another way, nearly a quarter of never-married 18- to 44-year-olds—3.9 million in all—have had at least one child.
>
> The uptick in single parenthood dates to the mid-1970s, when women started making enough money to support children without husbands, but the latest statistics underscore how widespread it has become.[1]

The point is, some are choosing to have babies alone. Some even select a man with certain genes to produce the kind of child they want—never mind God's standard of morality, or even what is best for the child. Medical technology aids and abets our inherent tendency toward willfulness. Choosing the sex of the child is now possible, and abortion is an evil convenience for women who insist, "I'm going to control my own body."

Christian women are not so likely to seek purposefully to give birth to a child out of wedlock, or to get an abortion. But many do exhibit headstrong ways in seeking friends, a job, a mate, a house, etc.—both for themselves and for their children. You may need to examine your own heart and ask yourself, "Am I yielding to God in every part of my life, or do I insist on keeping control myself in some areas?"

OK, LORD—BUT...

"OK, Lord, I'll stay here if that's what you want... but I'm sure not going to enjoy it!" Not exactly a prayer of humility and submission is it? But I (Ruthanne) actually said that to God at a time in my life when he wasn't answering my prayers in the way I wanted, and I had tried to make things happen on my own.

In my mid-twenties, I had completed three years of Bible college and made lots of friends, but where romance was concerned I always came up empty-handed. My idea of a solution was to leave that place and my secretarial job at the college—which I believed was a dead-end street leading to spinsterhood.

I tried to transfer to another college in a much larger city where I wanted to pursue a degree in writing, but was denied because my record was deficient in high school mathematics. I wrote to apply for a job with a Christian publisher; they didn't even answer my letter. Then a large church in the Midwest offered me a job as director of publications, and an open door to become a writer. It looked ideal, and I really wanted to accept it. Yet during my interview visit I had an uneasy feeling that something was not quite right.

Back at my campus apartment I prayed for direction; God's response was a clear "No." I reluctantly obeyed, but felt almost as if God were keeping me in bondage in a place where I didn't want to be, rather than guiding me in the way that was best. The truth is, I was bound by my own willfulness and wanting to do things my way. But I kept my job at the Bible college and went to school part-time to finish a degree, convinced it would be a miserable year. But God is merciful—even to his stubborn children.

A few weeks after school opened I met John, a new professor at the college and a widower with two children. Within a year he was my husband. I'd always wanted to marry someone who was tall and charming, and was a preacher or a professor—and John was all of them. That definitely was not a boring year!

Some time later the church that had offered me the publications job was rocked by a sex scandal involving the pastor's wife and several single young women in the church—one of whom was to have been my roommate. Had I insisted on doing things my way I could have been implicated in a very ugly situation. How grateful I am that the Lord managed to get my attention, and that

I had the wit to obey him even though it was with a poor attitude.

In the thirty years since then—as wife, mother, minister's wife, writer, and traveling teacher—I've learned some hard lessons. One is that God's ways truly are best for me, though they don't always seem to make logical sense at the time of his leading. Another is that trying to manipulate people and circumstances only leads to bondage.

The word manipulate means "to treat or operate with the hands; to change by artful, unfair or insidious means, especially to one's own advantage." When we yield to that tendency we are literally taking matters into our own hands. We are called to love people, pray for them, and perhaps on occasion offer counsel. But God's desire is that we entrust our own circumstances and our loved ones into his hands, knowing his wisdom is so much greater than ours.

NURTURING OR MANIPULATING?

Scripture teaches us to nurture our children in the ways of God, but how often we parents also want to choose our children's mates, or steer them onto the career path of our choice. For instance, a woman gives up a career for marriage, then tries to live out her frustrated dreams through a daughter by pushing her into that same career—never mind the child's innate talents or God's plan for her life. Fathers are sometimes guilty of the same behavior.

Much unhappiness and alienation in families can often be traced to a manipulative parent who tries to keep a child in bondage to the parent's own desires and goals—even worthy goals. One mother told us of her efforts to ensure that her son Tony made good grades in algebra. Fearful that he wouldn't do well on the final exam, she set up an appointment with a tutor to compensate for his inattention in class—even though Tony declared he wouldn't go. One day, as exam week was approaching, the mother was praying a paraphrase of Isaiah 54:13: "Thank you that my son will be taught by you, Lord, and great will be his peace."

Suddenly she heard the Lord speak quietly in her heart: "If you want me to be his teacher, then you get out of the way." She knew that Tony needed to learn to be responsible for his own choices, and that God was not pleased with her efforts to protect her son from himself. She cancelled the appointment with the tutor, stopped nagging Tony about his studies, and prayed, "Lord, I release this situation into your hands, and ask you to teach Tony the lessons he needs to learn. Thank you that you redeem our mistakes."

Sure enough, he failed the final exam and got a poor grade for the semester. A year later, that low mark kept Tony from being accepted at the university he desperately wanted to attend. It was a bitter lesson for him, and a sobering lesson for his mom. But God mercifully opened another door of opportunity for Tony's college education.

Quin knows a pastor who once admitted to his congregation that he was in the ministry because he had "a call from Mom" rather than a call from God. A college classmate of Ruthanne's was alienated from his family and his faith when his mother refused to accept the Christian young woman he wanted to marry.

Quin shares her own experience with this problem. "My mother, with four children to raise as a single parent, ran a boarding house. It seemed only natural to her that I, the eldest, should get a degree in hotel and restaurant management to be better equipped to help in the business. After a year of those miserable courses, I told Mom if I couldn't major in journalism, I might as well drop out of college. From the time I'd begun reporting news on the Girl Scouts for our local newspaper, writing had been my love.

"I reasoned with Mom that since I was working two jobs to pay my college tuition, I wanted to choose my own major. Thankfully, she agreed, and lived long enough to see me win the prestigious *Guideposts Magazine* writing contest, but not long enough to see my first book in print. I've always been grateful that she didn't insist on manipulating my career choice, and I've tried to follow her example with my own children."

A RELUCTANT BRIDE

Gail is a beautiful, thirty-something woman with a successful career in the fashion industry and admirable musical talent. A committed Christian, she is single, and she desires a husband and children of her own—a normal, God-given desire. But like Ruthanne, her frustration about the matter almost pushed her over the edge into a costly mistake.

Through her participation in a recording project, Gail met Mark, also a gospel musician. A whirlwind courtship followed, though they lived in different cities, and Mark soon proposed marriage. She accepted his engagement ring and they began making plans for an extravagant wedding. But it wasn't long before Mark began urging Gail to elope instead. "What's the big rush?" she asked, "I want us to have a real wedding." He said "his life was on hold" until they could be together, but he reluctantly agreed to wait for the wedding, and she agreed to move to his home in another state. Friends at her church gave them a huge shower. Three weeks before the wedding Gail leased out her apartment and Mark traveled the nine-hundred-plus miles that separated them to help her pack her belongings. It seemed so exciting to be starting a new life!

Yet in her private moments Gail had nagging feelings of doubt. During Mark's visit she was troubled, and at times embarrassed, by the way he interacted with her friends. In a social setting he would appear to be very generous, but behind the scenes she discovered he was less than honest.

After Mark left she tried to shake off her growing skepticism about him. "It's just because of so many changes coming so fast," she reasoned with herself. "Doesn't every bride get the prenuptial jitters?"

But she knew the Lord was quietly speaking to her heart, as he had been for several months. Tossing and turning through a sleepless night, Gail reviewed all the preparations that had been made for the wedding. Her bridal gown was ready and the bridesmaids' dresses ordered. She had sent out six hundred invitations and received scores of gifts. Friends had spent thousands of dollars on plane tickets to attend the big event.

As a new day dawned Gail prayed, "Lord, I know I could call it off—but it's too big. I just can't back out now—God, have mercy on me...." She rushed to shower, dress, and apply makeup to cover the circles under her eyes, then went on to the assignment to which she was committed for the next several days.

Later that day her world was turned upside down by a phone call. It was not from Mark, but from her pastor.

"Gail, I have some shocking news for you." Her pastor's familiar voice was tense and hesitant. "Mark's lawyer just called to tell me Mark has been arrested and is in serious legal trouble in relation to two young boys."

After a moment of dead silence, Gail found her voice. "Does it involve sexual charges?" she asked.

"Yes, it does," he said, "and these are very serious charges. I advise you not to try to contact Mark until we learn more about the situation."

Gail hung up the phone, feeling numb, shocked, and relieved all at the same time. It was over. She knew the wedding was off for good. Pulling the diamond ring off her finger, she called her parents and closest friends. Struggling to sort out her feelings of betrayal and anger, she had to find another place to live, retrieve her furniture and belongings, and begin putting her life back together. Another blow came when she learned police had been investigating the abuse charges for some time, and Mark had known about it from the very month he had proposed to her.

"Then I understood why he had pressed me to elope," she said. "He apparently felt that if he were married to someone like me, it would make him look good.

"What was your greatest disappointment?" I asked. "Realizing Mark had deceived you and was actually using you?"

"No," Gail answered, shaking her head. "My greatest disappointment was in myself—that I did not pay attention to the Holy Spirit. I knew all along that this man was not God's best for me. I never felt peace about marrying him, but I wanted so badly to have a loving relationship with a man. In the past people had said I was too picky—that I expected too much in a guy. 'Everyone has to work out problems in their marriage,' I told myself. 'Why should Mark and I be any different? We can work things out.'"

Now, many months beyond the trauma and its aftermath, Gail is very grateful that Mark's problems came to light before the wedding took place. The charges against him are still pending, with trial dates repeatedly delayed. She has forgiven him, and the relationship definitely is a closed chapter in her life.

"Even though I refused to heed his warnings, God allowed circumstances to close the door on what I was about to do," she shared. "Thank God, he protected me from myself. I've learned the hard way that my relationship with him must be first in my life, and I'm not allowing anything to distract me from that. Someday I hope to marry and have children, but I've given those desires to the Lord. It has to be God's plan, not my own."

A SOBER WARNING

Gail's story illustrates God's merciful intervention to protect her from the consequences of a bad decision. Otherwise she could have ended up in the bondage of disappointment, within a possibly abusive marriage. If this is sobering to you, we pray you will heed it as a warning. Far better to avoid bondage when possible than to struggle later to escape it.

In one sense, wanting our own way is the problem women began with in the Garden of Eden, which led to alienation between God and his people. Our desire to control or manipulate circumstances and people can become a pattern of behavior which may keep us from intimacy with God, and ultimately lead to bondage. It is one of the biggest hindrances to freedom in the Spirit.

Many women who've talked to us admit choosing their own way over the good of others and the wisdom of God, often going against inner warnings or wise counsel. Now they face painful consequences such as financial loss or joblessness, broken relationships with family members, a difficult marriage, divorce, or the problem of rearing an out-of-wedlock child. How best to deal with these crushing problems?

First, confess to the Lord your sin of willfulness and fully repent before him. This is a time to take full responsibility for your part in the matter, without shifting the blame to someone else.

Next, ask God to redeem your mistakes. His love and mercy can transform even the most hopeless circumstances into something positive and fruitful. The key is in being willing to submit to his ways, to receive his forgiveness for your mistakes, and to forgive yourself.

Then, submit your ways to God's ways and observe this admonition Jesus gives:

> If anyone would come after me, he must deny himself and take up his cross daily and follow me. For whoever wants to save his life will lose it, but whoever loses his life for me will save it. What good is it for a man to gain the whole world, and yet lose or forfeit his very self? **Luke 9:23-25**

"Are you asking me to give up my rights?" you may ask. Yes, essentially, that is exactly what the Christian life means. But giving up your own "rights" means you now "have a right to Christ," as author Mabel Williamson says. She concludes her excellent book, *Have We No Rights?* with this:

> All that He takes I will give;
> All that He gives will I take;

He, my only right!
He, the one right before which all other rights fade into nothingness.
I have full right to Him;
Oh, may He have full right to me![2]

PRAYER

Lord, I repent for insisting upon my own way and trying to run my own life, or someone else's. Forgive me for thinking I know better than you. Help me learn to take "hands off"—trusting you with the plan and purpose you have for me, and for my loved ones. I don't want to be a Jezebel. I don't want to have selfish ambition for myself, my child, my spouse, my parents, or anyone close to me.

Lord, break this thing in me that wants to control and manipulate. Forgive me for trying to put other people into bondage with my desires, or even with the words I've spoken against them when they didn't choose "my way." Help me, by the power of the Holy Spirit, to walk this out every day, and please remind me when I fall back into the old pattern. Lord, I truly repent and desire to change. Your way is so much better than mine! I choose your way, in Jesus' name. Amen.

SIX

Freedom from Rejection and Abuse

Though my father and mother forsake me, the Lord will receive me. Teach me your way, O Lord; lead me in a straight path because of my oppressors.

Psalm 27:10-11

Victims of sexual, physical, and emotional abuse fill hospitals, divorce courts, and psychiatrists' offices. Victims of abuse often repress the memories of the ill treatment they have suffered because the pain is too great to retain in conscious memory.

Whether remembered consciously or not, however, abuse creates bondage in its victim. Those who suffered abuse in childhood carry the repressed memories into adulthood. They begin to realize something is wrong when they have problems with functioning normally in life and establishing healthy relationships. They sometimes tend to manipulate and control those around them, and often have difficulty trusting others, especially those in authority. These defense mechanisms are simply the victim's way of keeping people at arm's length and trying to avoid further abuse.

Christian psychologist Dr. H. Norman Wright defines abuse as being "any behavior designed to control and/or subjugate another person through the use of fear, humiliation, and verbal or physical assaults. Humiliating, making fun of and putting down a child or even a spouse can be abusive."[1]

LITANY OF ABUSE

Marsha's story of abuse is an all-too-familiar litany of rejection, neglect, fear, and pain, which reveals how abuse can lead to the bondage of depression and anger. Problems in her marriage were clearly connected to the abuse she had suffered, though she had repressed memories of it. But her story also shows us how God's acceptance, love, nurture, and healing—the fulfillment of the above verses from Psalm 27—can transform a life.

"Through counseling and his Word—the ultimate counselor—God has begun to heal my pain and wounds from a childhood filled with abuse," shares this slender, dark-haired flight attendant. "It is only through the 'uncovering' that I have been able to 'recover' and turn from the dominion of Satan to God."

For Marsha, as with many women, she didn't truly become aware of the effects of her abuse until after she was married. She became a Christian at age twenty-one and was married a year later to the young man who had drawn her to the Lord.

"Right after we were married I began to fall apart," she reported. "Depression, anger, lack of sexual desire... these were my symptoms. Suddenly the man I had chosen to marry was a thorn in my side. Everthing he did bothered me, and everything he didn't do bothered me worse. This drove me to seek professional help from a Christian psychologist, and thus began the long journey and 'battle' of uncovering the darkness of my past. The Scripture says, 'He will bring to light what is hidden in darkness...' (1 Cor 4:5b), and that's exactly what the Lord has done."

NEVER GOOD ENOUGH

The last of three children born to an unhappily married couple, Marsha's earliest memories are of feeling sad, lonely, abandoned, and afraid. Of striving to win approval and affection from her alcoholic parents, but never succeeding and never understanding why. Of wishing she could be like her older sister so that her mother would love her.

"Once while sitting at the dinner table when I was about six, my father went into a rage and tried to hit my older brother in the head with a beer bottle," she shared. "I was terrified, and left the table. Later, my mother said I was good because I didn't say anything; it's the only time I ever remember her giving me a compliment. The incident was quite frightening. Afterward I kept repeating to myself over and over, 'But I was good because I didn't say anything.'

"I'm sure my mother never wanted me to be born; she always made me feel 'put down' no matter what I did. She would leave me alone at night to go to a bar, then bring strange men home with her and sleep with them. One of her forms of punishment was to beat me and lock me in a closet or in my room. She seemed to give more attention to the neighbors' girls than to me, so I felt I was not good enough to be loved. When I performed in my first and only ballet recital, she wouldn't even come to see me. I don't have a single happy memory with my mother—but I always wished she would love me, take care of me, and show her love through a kiss, a hug, or a smile.

"From the time I was little until my parents divorced when I was eight years old, my father sexually abused me—his only interest in me was for his own pleasure. The only other times he noticed me was to criticize me or belittle my efforts to please him. The long-term effect of this was that his example of parenting became my example of God. I was filled with shame, fear, and anger."

Author Nancy Groom explains the damage a child suffers as a result of this kind of treatment:

> When parents fail to minister grace to their children, to esteem and value them as precious for their own sakes, children absorb the shame of their inadequacies into their deepest images of themselves. This shame does damage far beyond the original

> dysfunction because it is damage they unintentionally continue to perpetrate on themselves... 'a kind of soul murder.' When a child's dependency needs are not satisfied by his parents, the damage to his soul is penetrating and longlasting.[2]

Marsha's healing began when she remembered the most significant events of her past which she had repressed. Through counseling and prayer she began to understand what had happened, how it had affected her life, and why she responded to life as she did. She began to realize the depth of God's love for her—that he did not will for her to suffer abuse, that he had preserved her in spite of it. She began to revise her distorted image of God that had been shaped by her father's sinful behavior.

Marsha tried to talk to her mother about the pain of her childhood, but ran headlong into a wall of denial as her mother refused to talk to her. A discussion with her brother and sister confirmed that the abuse by both her parents had indeed happened, which gave her confidence that she wasn't imagining things. With the counselor's help she began to accept the reality that her mother would never "be there" for her—the most difficult stage of the process. But in Marsha's case it caused her to run into God's arms and seek from him the nurture and affirmation she had missed all her life.

Her deep disappointment and anger had to find expression, so she wrote her mother a letter but purposely never mailed it. Because of her love for God, and in obedience to him, she willed to forgive her mother, then began moving through the stages of grief. Unexpectedly, she received notification from a mortuary in the state where her mother lived that her mother had died, and had stipulated that there was to be no funeral.

LIGHT AND HEALING

As she prayed Marsha felt the Lord leading her to have a "burial ceremony" in her home to bring closure to this area of her life. With her husband, the counselor, her pastor, and another friend present, she read several Scriptures. Among them was Isaiah 49:15-16, a passage that had given her much comfort:

> Can a mother forget the baby at her breast and have no compassion on the child she has borne? Though she may forget, I will not forget you! See, I have engraved you on the palms of my hands; your walls are ever before me.

She prayed, "Lord, thank you that when you engraved me on the palms of your hands, it was with nail prints. Thank you for dying for me; I know you died for my parents too. Lord, take all of me and mend all the holes in my heart." Then she burned the mortuary notification paper as a symbol of releasing her mother into God's hands.

"Marsha, all your life you have grieved for the mother you longed for but never had," her pastor said. "Normally a service like this marks the beginning of grief; today we are marking the end of that grief for you."

Marsha concluded: "When it is told, I want this dark story to bring light and healing to others."

Although her mother's lifelong abuse was the most difficult to deal with, Marsha also had to face the memories of her father's abuse. She wrote him a letter (and mailed it) and again hit a wall of denial. But God has enabled her to forgive him, release him, and put it behind her. Her husband has been very supportive, and their relationship is being healed and strengthened. Marsha is grateful to God for the gift of her two little boys, knowing he will enable her truly to love them as she had longed to be loved.

ABUSIVE HUSBANDS

An abused child like Marsha is trapped in the situation and seldom has a way of escape unless a teacher or other authority figure intervenes. Wives with abusive husbands, however, can take action to protect themselves. We do not feel any woman should subjugate herself to abuse of any kind—verbal, emotional, physical, or sexual.

According to a report by the U.S. Justice Department, two-thirds of the women who are victims of violent crimes are attacked by a husband, a boyfriend, a relative, or an acquaintance, based on a four-year survey of 400,000 women. Another report says as many as 30 percent of women who visit emergency rooms each year are victims of domestic violence. Statistics indicate that women who grew up with abuse very often end up marrying abusive husbands.

Emotional abuse in a marriage relationship can be one of the most painful experiences a woman ever endures. You begin your marriage with commitment and dreams for the future, but often disillusionment settles in when you realize other interests in your husband's life mean more to him than you do. You feel a sense of rejection and emotional separation. Then come the put-downs and verbal assaults, and your self-esteem withers and dies. Almost unconsciously, you find you're in bondage to a lifetime of fear, shame, and unresolved and repressed anger. The following letter from a reader is a picture of a woman being manipulated by an emotionally abusive husband.

> My husband Anthony and I have been separated and living apart on and off for three years. I am a Christian and don't believe in divorce. My husband is not a Christian; divorce runs in his family. He recently filed for divorce and has requested custody of our six-year-old son David (we currently have 50/50 custody).
>
> Anthony has a girlfriend and has been sleeping with her, even when David is staying with him for a visit. I still love my husband and have remained faithful and I never turn him away. I know there is still a part of him that cares about me because we usually talk at least once each day and we still make love about once a week.
>
> He and his girlfriend are involved in New Age healing and

philosophies. Anthony has had out-of-body experiences and has been visited by "entities" as he calls them (I call them demons!). Of course, my son is often rebellious and defiant toward me and his teachers at the Christian day care center. I am also battered by Satan continuously and I'm under attack on my job. I feel like I'm about to lose my mind. I pray the divorce never happens.

This woman, gripped by the fear of an impending divorce, fails to see that she is allowing her husband to emotionally abuse her. By granting him sex while he's also sleeping with his girlfriend, she gives tacit approval to his adulterous behavior, puts her own safety in jeopardy, and keeps herself in bondage to his control. What are her options?

First, she needs to refuse sexual contact with Anthony and force him to choose between her and the other woman. This is difficult to do, but necessary if she is to regain her self-esteem and respect. Then she needs to release her husband by forgiving him for his unfaithfulness, and telling him she has done this. And last, she must depend upon God's help to vindicate her and help her retain custody of her son.

ABUSE ON THE JOB

Rejection and abuse happen not only in families, but at the workplace as well. In fact, abuse victims—if they don't receive help and achieve integration in their lives—usually become abusers. They abuse their own children as well as fellow employees who work under their supervision on the job.

Joyce is a friend who finally left her husband because of his abusive behavior toward her and her two daughters. She returned to nursing after being out of the medical work force for several years, but she quickly realized she had left one abusive relationship and walked into another on her job.

"Every day, from the moment I stepped off the elevator on the third floor of the hospital until I went home, I was engaged in a spiritual battle," Joyce shared. "Barbara, the head nurse of our psychiatric unit, obviously felt threatened by me. I had more credentials than she did, though she had lots of seniority, and she was furious because her boss had hired me for her unit. She vented her rage by attacking everything I did.

"If my work was done on time and in an organized way, she said I was 'compulsive.' If I didn't get my work done on time or to her satisfaction, she called me 'ineffective.' She made hateful remarks to me and criticized the way I walked, the way I related to the patients, the way I related to other staff members.

"She stood six feet tall and was slightly heavy—almost twice my size—so it was easy to feel intimidated by her. Judging by her seething, pent-up anger, I think she surely must be an abuse victim. For years I had battled intimidation and control in my husband. Now I was fighting the same demonic behavior in my supervisor. I knew this was more than just a personality conflict or working for a tough boss—I was dealing with entrenched spiritual bondages in this woman."

Every morning during her thirty-minute drive to work, Joyce held her Bible on her lap and prayed unceasingly. She prayed several key Scriptures every day, such as these:

> How great is your goodness,
> Which you have stored up for those who fear you,
> Which you bestow in the sight of men
>   on those who take refuge in you.
> In the shelter of your presence you hide them
>   from the intrigues of men;
> In your dwelling you keep them safe from accusing tongues.
> Praise be to the Lord,
> For he showed his wonderful love to me
>   when I was in a besieged city. **Psalm 31:19-21**

You are my hiding place;
you will protect me from trouble
and surround me with songs of deliverance. **Psalm 32:7**

"I constantly fought exhaustion, anxiety, tension, fear, and condemnation while working with this woman," Joyce reported. "She was abusive to me, to other staff members, and occasionally to patients. I felt safer with the patients in this psychiatric setting than I did in the nurses' station with Barbara. Other workers often talked about her behind her back, but they were afraid to confront her or to 'tell on her.' The story of Joseph's dungeon experience was my encouragement through many stormy days. I tried to follow his pattern of behavior while 'in prison' on my job. My prayer partner and I prayed for Barbara's salvation, but I could not penetrate her bitterness to share the gospel with her."

Joyce had to work, so quitting was not an option. She knew it was imperative that she forgive Barbara, because harboring unforgiveness, resentment, and anger would block her walk with the Lord.

"Daily, before I got to work, I would pray for protection, pray my Scriptures, and willfully declare, 'Barbara, you are forgiven.' I tried to speak kind words to her without letting her walk all over me. I didn't want to respond to her in the same spirit she was operating in.

"Many times throughout the day I'd have to find a quiet, private place and pray a quick prayer: 'I forgive you, Barbara.' On one occasion the Lord spoke to me through Proverbs 21:14a ('A gift given in secret soothes anger,') and told me to bless her with a gift, which I did. She was obviously touched and mellowed for a couple of days."

Joyce had been on the job almost a year when she had an unusual dream. She saw Barbara fallen flat on her face and utterly helpless. She felt the Lord was assuring her that Barbara would soon be gone.

"Four months later another staff R.N. and I had a divinely

arranged opportunity to speak to the two head administrative people about Barbara," Joyce shared. "We were able to document the abuses we had observed and experienced; they were shocked to realize this had been going on without their knowledge. Within twenty-four hours, Barbara was no longer on the job. I never found out whether she was transferred to another unit, or simply fired. But I pray the conviction of the Holy Spirit will follow her wherever she goes. I believe obeying the Word regarding forgiveness, blessing my oppressor, and standing on his promises of deliverance paved the way for my freedom from that bondage of abuse."

WORDS THAT DAMAGE THE SOUL

As children we used to chant to our playmates after a name-calling dispute, "Sticks and stones may break my bones, but words can never harm me." That is a lie. Words don't leave bruises and black eyes, but they can do profound damage to the soul.

Words of rejection spoken to you and about you function like the recording head of an old-fashioned phonograph. The "message" is transmitted via a needle which cuts a series of grooves into the soft material of the phonograph record, which then hardens. Every time you play the record you hear a "less than" message. You're not good enough, smart enough, pretty enough, talented enough, diligent enough... to be accepted by your family and peers. And so you begin to see yourself as "less than" others.

Dr. Grace Ketterman, author of *Verbal Abuse: Healing the Hidden Wound,* writes:

> Verbal abuse is any statement to a victim that results in emotional damage. Such damage limits his or her happiness and productivity for a lifetime.... In essence, verbal abuse creates emotional scars that may permanently disfigure a person.... Emotional scars, while leaving a permanent mark on the soul, can also serve a useful purpose. They are reminders of the lessons we can learn from painful experiences. They are symbols of a healthy toughness we can acquire, once we understand ver-

bal abuse. Our emotional scars remind us to learn and use greater control over our feelings and how we react to abuse from others. That sense of self-control is, after all, what we all have. We can rarely, if ever, control others. But we can always decide how we respond to them![3]

Have you ever considered the power that words have to keep us in bondage? Joyce's story illustrates how her supervisor's hateful words literally were like a barrage of gunfire aimed at her every day on the job. Had she not resisted and approached the problem as a spiritual battle, she would have ended up in bondage, speaking and acting toward others the same way Barbara did. And her "self-talk" would have reinforced all the evil things Barbara had spoken against her.

Whether we talk to ourselves or others, speaking evil or negative words that do not agree with God's Word can create bondage. Words that others speak about us or write against us—if we agree with them—keep us in bondage!

Scripture says, "There is one who speaks rashly like the thrusts of a sword, but the tongue of the wise brings healing" (Prv 12:18, NASB). Also, "Death and life are in the power of the tongue" (Prv 18:21a, NASB). Our spoken words can be blessings or curses—to heal or to hurt.

Word curses are very real. Jesus spoke to a fig tree and it withered (Mk 11:14, 21). Joshua cursed the rebuilding of Jericho, saying anyone who did rebuild it would lose his firstborn and youngest sons. Five hundred years later it came about exactly as he had said (see Joshua 6:26 and 1 Kings 16:34).

VERBAL ABUSE CAN BE A "WORD CURSE"

To curse is to invoke evil or injury upon someone, to wish upon that person calamity or evil such as injury.

A curse can take the form of negative expectations—like a parent who judges a child for failing, for "being dumb," for "being different," or for not measuring up.

My friend Will's mother said to him over and over, "Son, you were always poor and you will always be poor." In his early fifties, he lost his business and had to start all over again.

Lynn's mom used to tell her, "You will someday have a daughter just like you—incorrigible." And she did.

Debbie often described her twelve-year-old son to others by saying, "He's been difficult since birth." He lived up to her words, until she repented and asked his forgiveness.

Seventy-year-old Dorothy shares her testimony to illustrate that verbal abuse is actually like a word curse. Her story also illustrates the tendency of abuse victims to marry abusive men:

> My two marriages ended for the same reasons: verbal, mental, and physical abuse. I married to get out from under my mom's constant mental torment. She called me a brat and a failure and compared me with anyone she could think of who was rotten. I felt put down and unaccepted by others. I did not expect them to like me—after all, I was not as "smart" as they were. I thought I was a failure!
>
> After my marriages failed I had three children to raise by myself. I literally put my life on hold and worked to see the children grow up. But since I've found Christ, received the Holy Spirit, and with his help forgiven Mom, my life has changed.
>
> Now ninety-two years old, Mom still calls me a brat. I don't see her often, but I love her and am sorry for her. I can only trust the Lord to do a work in her and in my daughter, whom Mom poisoned against me with her bitter words. I am walking in victory—no longer in bondage to the words she has spoken over me.

BLESS, DON'T CURSE

Words can also bless us. Consider the words God gave to be spoken over the ancient Israelites:

> The Lord said to Moses, "Tell Aaron and his sons, 'This is how you are to bless the Israelites. Say to them: ""The Lord bless you and keep you; the Lord make his face shine upon you and be gracious to you; the Lord turn his face toward you and give you peace."'" **Numbers 6:22-26**

From Old Testament times to now, the tradition of the Jewish father to bless his children has been an important part of Jewish family life. In *The Family Blessing*, Rolf Garborg, a Christian parent who blesses his children every day, writes:

> As the ancient Hebrews recognized, words of blessings spoken in the name of God are somehow able to transmit the power and favor of God. This is simply a mystery which we must accept, and for which we must be grateful. However the blessing works, those who have faithfully spoken it year after year would probably all agree on one point: We practice the family blessing because it is right. And because it is right, God rewards those who bless.[4]

In the stories of rejection and abuse shared in this chapter we see the significance of spoken words and the consequences they produce—for evil or good, for hurt or blessing. If you are struggling with the bondage of words spoken over you, begin your way to freedom by using Scripture to break the power of those words. Read aloud to yourself the Scriptures we share in the following chapter that reinforce how precious, treasured, and loved you are in God's sight.

TO BREAK A CURSE

To break a word curse over yourself or a loved one, you can pray a paraphrase of Isaiah 54:17: "No weapon formed against (name of victim) shall prosper, and every tongue that accuses (him/her/me) in judgment will be condemned. This is the heritage of the servants of the Lord, and their vindication is from the Lord" (NASB).

PRAYER FOR ABUSE VICTIM

Lord Jesus, you knew rejection, abandonment, pain, and betrayal by those close to you. So you can identify with my hurts and wounds. Yet, Lord, as you hung on that cross, bleeding and dying from wounds you didn't deserve, you actually asked your Father to forgive your offenders. Lord, please help me to forgive each person who has abused, rejected, or cursed me. Right now I honestly don't feel some of them deserve forgiveness. But because I want my relationship with you to be right, I choose to forgive and set myself free.

Lord, I ask you to heal my painful memories. Help me to anticipate with joy what you have in store for my life, now that I'm on the road to healing. Your Word says you complete the work you start.[5] *Thank you that you will finish my healing, and that you will never leave me nor forsake me. Amen.*

SEVEN

Freedom from Shame and Guilt

Instead of your shame you will have a double portion and instead of humiliation they will shout for joy over their portion. **Isaiah 61:7a, NASB**

Shame relates to how we feel about ourselves—our self-image. Guilt is the sense of regret we feel about something we did—our behavior. Shame in the Bible is depicted as disgrace, dishonor, and nakedness.

"For as long as I can remember, I felt inferior to other people, and I never felt I could trust anyone," Corrie shared with us over lunch one day. "It was very difficult for me to accept a gift from anyone; I always suspected an ulterior motive. Several months ago I began having troubling dreams about being raped, and I was overreacting in anger toward my husband.

"Finally I got help from a counselor and began to remember the details of being raped when I was about four years old by a friend of my uncle who enticed me with a gift. Shame, guilt, and fear began to surface as the counselor worked with me. But as I began to express my feelings and allow myself to be open to the Holy Spirit's work in my heart, healing began.

"One day during the process of my healing I saw a mental

image of myself kneeling before the Lord. My head was bowed and I was wearing a dark cloak. Jesus reached out to me, lifted off the dark cloak, and underneath I saw that I was wearing a white robe of righteousness. That dark cloak was the shame I had been wearing since childhood. As Jesus lifted it off I felt such a release, such joy! It was a turning point in my life that has helped my relationship with the Lord, with my husband and children, and with other people."

Corrie's experience is a graphic example of the tremendous impact shame can have upon your life. In fact, in her case it could well be called "toxic shame." Even after she received Christ and knew she had received his righteousness, a cloak of shame kept her from feeling truly accepted and loved by him. She never felt she could trust him.

"NATURAL" VS. "TOXIC" SHAME

Professional therapists distinguish between natural shame and damaging shame such as Corrie struggled with. Pia Mellody, an abuse victim who is now a counselor, writes:

> We experience natural shame as a mild to moderate feeling of embarrassment when we notice ourselves making a mistake or being imperfect.... Shame "notifies" our conscious mind that we have made a mistake, and we need to correct it or to stop doing whatever we're doing, because it's not appropriate.
>
> ... I consider shame to be both a gift from God and a legacy of abuse. When it's a gift from God, the experience of our own natural shame makes us aware that we are fallible. But shame as a legacy of abuse has to do with the devastating and crippling experience of carried or induced shame because it is this shame that diminishes our sense of our inherent worth, making us feel less than others.
>
> ... It's not a matter of just feeling imperfect and accountable

> (as we do with natural shame). We feel a much deeper experience of "less than." We may feel mortified, worthless, and horrible about ourselves.[1]

Pia Mellody explains that when an irresponsible caregiver abuses a child, he (or she) is denying his own shame, and that burden of shame passes to the child. It's like giving a little girl a huge overloaded suitcase to carry, then causing her to feel inadequate because she can't manage the task! Pia continues:

> Children's internal boundary systems are not fully developed and they cannot keep from taking on the feelings of the adult offender.
>
> ... Shame is the primary feeling passed to the child. I believe this because it is "shameless" to abuse a defenseless child. A shameless person is one who is denying his or her own shame, which passes directly to the child. The child's own shame gives him or her a sense of fallibility, but adding the parent's [or abuser's] shame to the child's shame gives the child an overwhelming sense of worthlessness, "badness," and inadequacy.
>
> ... In a functional system parents are accountable when they fail to be there for the child. The parents experience their imperfectness—and natural shame—and make amends to the child...
>
> But when the parents in a dysfunctional system repeatedly deny their own feelings, or are irresponsible with their own feelings of shame, the child... develops a core of induced shame as a result (which I call a "shame core") that *constantly* tells the child (and later adult) that he or she has less value than other people.
>
> This message, "You have less value than others," forms the basis for the first symptom of codependence, difficulty experiencing appropriate levels of self-esteem, and is, I believe, the heart of codependence. And this is why codependence is called a shame-based disease.[2]

SHAME DAMAGES SELF-ESTEEM

A woman who has such a core of toxic (transferred) shame inevitably will struggle with her sense of self-esteem. The message that plays over and over in her head is, "You're no good... you'll never amount to anything... people think you're weird."

Counselors see women who respond to this core of shame in a variety of ways:

- denying their shame by plunging headlong into a promiscuous lifestyle
- becoming substance-addicted in an attempt to medicate their pain
- refusing to give attention to self-care—unkempt hair, poor personal grooming, slumped posture, overweight
- jogging and exercising excessively, consumed with excelling in sports
- isolating themselves, refusing to become involved in close relationships
- compulsively seeking approval from others—especially men—to feel a sense of self-worth
- striving to excel at everything they do to validate their existence
- becoming a "crusader" for the helpless—feeding homeless children and the like
- becoming "control freaks" obsessed with controlling people and circumstances in their environment
- getting involved in lesbian relationships as a result of their hatred of men
- developing an eating disorder.

Inevitably, these women run out of steam to maintain their carefully constructed survival system. They ask for help. Sometimes their cries are silent, but with spiritual perception you can see the pain in their eyes. You may be one of them. You probably rub shoulders with women like this every day.

REJECTION FROM THE WOMB

Christy's story is a picture of how the seeds of rejection produce a dysfunctional adult who is in bondage to shame. Her mother, Rena, got pregnant with her in a desperate attempt to keep her husband from walking out on her. The scheme failed and he left anyway. At this point she decided she didn't want to have the baby. Abortion was illegal, so she plotted another scheme. Hearing of an acquaintance who had German measles, she invited this person over and purposely exposed herself to the disease in the hope it would cause her to miscarry. This plan also failed. Christy was born, but she's almost completely blind in one eye.

During childhood her surroundings were filled with arguing, name-calling, shouting, and beatings. The father who walked out came back, but he was violent and abusive. She lacked necessities such as basic school supplies, clean clothing, and nourishing food, and she was often ashamed to go to school because of her dirty clothes. A painful memory was of watching a beauty pageant on TV with her father and younger sister Jill when she was eight years old. When she spoke of her hopes of being in a pageant someday, her father laughed scornfully and said, "If anyone in our family is ever in one, it will be Jill."

Rena's behavior continually reinforced the message to Christy, "You're not worth anything—I wish you'd never been born." Her mother frequently slapped her, beat her with a hairbrush, and yanked her around by grabbing her hair. Sometimes she would lock Christy and her sisters outside so she and her husband or a boyfriend could have sex undisturbed. The children suffered from thirst and hunger, and would have to go to the bathroom outside.

Rena divorced and remarried two different times, and both stepfathers abused Christy physically, emotionally, and sexually. At age fifteen, when she was in a car accident with her mother driving, Christy was appalled that Rena never even bothered to ask whether she had been hurt. For the first time the full impact of the truth hit her: "Mom doesn't care about me at all." After a bitter fight, Christy ran away to live with relatives in another city.

That crisis proved to be a turning point, because her aunt and uncle took care of her and led her to Christ. Several years later she married and soon had a child of her own. It was after the birth of her baby that the ugly memories of her childhood began to surface. Christy sought counseling, and began peeling off the layers of rejection and shame that had accumulated since before she was born.

GOD WANTED YOU TO BE BORN

Her greatest struggle was reaching the point of feeling she had a right to exist. Her mother had tried to kill her while she was in the womb. As a teenager she'd had a horrendous experience when a Ouija board gave her the message she would die when she reached age thirty-two. When the memory of her occult involvement surfaced, the counselor immediately bound the spirit of death trying to destroy Christy, and broke the curse of death over her. (See chapters six and twelve for discussion on this topic.)

The counselor helped Christy realize that she is precious to God by having her study Psalm 139:13-16: "For you created my inmost being; you knit me together in my mother's womb. I praise you because I am fearfully and wonderfully made; your works are wonderful, I know that full well. My frame was not hidden from you when I was made in the secret place. When I was woven together in the depths of the earth, your eyes saw my unformed body. All the days ordained for me were written in your book before one of them came to be."

"You see, even though your mother didn't want you, God wanted you to be born," the counselor explained. "He protected your life when she wanted to abort you. Christy, he even named you after his son, Jesus Christ. Your name is a constant reminder that you are his beloved child."

The counselor then gave Christy an assignment to declare repeatedly, "I will to live! I had a right to be born, and I have a right to exist." At last the core of shame that had dominated her personality was broken up. From that time she began acting like an adult instead of a victimized child. She decided, by an act of her will, to forgive her mother, her father, and her stepfathers. All attempts to confront these people have been rebuffed, but Christy has not allowed that to deter her from moving toward complete healing. Her marriage is getting stronger as she and her husband are in counseling together. These verses are her testimony:

> I sought the Lord, and he answered me;
>   he delivered me from all my fears.
> Those who look to him are radiant;
>   their faces are never covered with shame. **Psalm 34:4-5**

GET IN TOUCH WITH TRUTH

"I was in bondage to something, but I didn't know what it was," wrote Nancy, one of our readers. "Now I'm being set free in the area of toxic shame—unhealthy shame. The Lord showed me I was stuck behind not being able to receive love. I never really believed anyone, including my husband, when they said they loved me."

Nancy, like scores of women we've met, grew up in a family with an alcoholic father. His drinking and angry rages, contrasted with his perfectionism and unreasonable demands, marked her with shame.

"I'm beginning to realize, as the Holy Spirit brings it to light, that my shame was not for what I did, but for who I was. Never perfect enough, educated enough, pretty enough, smart enough, n enough. Lots of guilt. Double-mindedness resulted.

"I read somewhere, 'Don't try to get in touch with your feelings; get in touch with truth and your feelings will change.' Now, when I hear shame trying to rule, I hear the Holy Spirit say, 'No shame, no shame!' I could never earn God's love, but I cannot be separated from his love. One verse that comforts me is, 'He heals the brokenhearted and binds up their wounds [curing their pains and sorrows]'" (Ps 147:3).

NO LONGER A VICTIM

We want you to see that you are not a hopeless victim. You can be free from shame's bondage. It may seem impossible to you to change the way you feel and the way you perceive yourself. But freedom is available if you cooperate with God. These are five helpful steps you can take:

1. Learn self-esteem from within. See yourself as God sees you, based on Scripture. Ask him to reveal this truth to you.

2. Establish healthy boundaries. Don't allow anyone to violate your body or your self-esteem. As you begin to respect yourself and see yourself as God sees you, your demeanor will command the respect of others.

3. Get in touch with your own feelings; get to know yourself and your personality. Discover your talents and exercise them. Show respect for your body by establishing good grooming and health habits. Take the risk of learning whom you can trust as friends, and how to respond to others socially.

4. Work toward becoming interdependent with other people in your life. Don't isolate yourself but don't be helplessly dependent upon others (see 1 Corinthians 12:21-27).

5. Live moderately—strike a balance between emotional highs and plunges into depression. Allow yourself to make mistakes and learn from them, without presuming you're a bad person because of a blunder.[3]

It is important to keep in mind that *you* are an object of God's love. Because he gave his son Jesus to die for you to free you from sin, you are infinitely valuable to him. These verses of Scripture reveal this fact:

> But he was pierced for our transgressions,
> he was crushed for our iniquities;
> the punishment that brought us peace was upon him,
> and by his wounds we are healed. **Isiah 53:5**

> You see, at just the right time, when we were still powerless, Christ died for the ungodly. Very rarely will anyone die for a righteous man, though for a good man someone might possibly dare to die. But God demonstrates his own love for us in this: While we were still sinners, Christ died for us. **Romans 5:6-8**

> He who did not spare his own Son, but gave him up for us all—how will he not also, along with him, graciously give us all things? **Romans 8:32**

> But because of his great love for us, God, who is rich in mercy, made us alive with Christ even when we were dead in transgressions—it is by grace you have been saved. **Ephesians 2:4-5**

THE VALUE OF GUILT AND REPENTANCE

We mentioned earlier that shame has to do with how we feel about ourselves, and guilt about our behavior. Our conscience troubles us when we've done wrong, and we feel guilty. You may, because of your upbringing, have a super-sensitive conscience that causes you to feel guilty about relatively minor matters. Or you may have a hardened conscience because of repeated wrongdoing. Scripture tells us: "To the pure, all things are pure, but to those who are corrupted and do not believe, nothing is pure. In fact, both their minds and consciences are corrupted" (Ti 1:15).

Though some secular psychiatrists such as Sigmund Freud teach that guilt is bad, it actually has a healthy role in your life if you respond to it appropriately by repenting for violating God's moral laws. However, once you repent and receive God's forgiveness, guilt has no reason to remain.

Many people seem to feel God's standards are unreasonably high, and they feel guilty and fearful that they can never measure up. It's true, we can never measure up in our own strength. But, as the late teacher A.W. Tozer reminds us:

> The truth is that God is the most winsome of all beings.... He is all love, and those who trust Him need never know anything but that love. He is just, indeed, and He will not condone sin; but through the blood of the everlasting covenant He is able to act toward us exactly as if we had never sinned.
>
> ... Some of us are religiously jumpy and self-conscious because we know that God sees our every thought and is acquainted with all our ways. We need not be. God is the sum of all patience and the essence of kindly good will.
>
> We please Him most, not by frantically trying to make ourselves good, but by throwing ourselves into His arms with all our imperfections, and believing that He understands everything and loves us still.[4]

NO STONE-THROWERS

We see an example of this from the life of Christ. Once when he was teaching a group of people in the temple, the teachers of the law brought before him a woman caught in the act of adultery—a sin punishable by death, according to Old Testament law. They asked Jesus what should be done with her, their motive being to trap him in an embarrassing dilemma before the people. Showing no compassion for the woman, they forced her to stand before the crowd in shame and humiliation.

Jesus did not accuse the woman. She obviously knew she had sinned, and knew she deserved punishment. Instead, he silently bent over and began writing on the ground while the self-righteous teachers pelted him with questions. When he stood up and spoke he nailed them with this challenge: "If any one of you is without sin, let him be the first to throw a stone at her" (Jn 8:7b).

As Jesus again bent over to write on the ground—perhaps in that culture a way of showing intentional disregard for one's accusers—each man who had denounced the woman walked away. When Jesus asked the woman whether anyone had judged her gullty, she replied, "No one, Lord."

Jesus responded, "Then neither do I condemn you.... Go now and leave your life of sin" (Jn 8:11b).

We aren't told of the woman's reaction. But surely after seeing her accusers walk away, then having Jesus remove her shame and guilt, she must have followed him with gratitude.

After receiving God's forgiveness, as this woman did, you must also forgive yourself if you are truly to be free from guilt. Otherwise "false guilt" turns inward and produces anger toward yourself. Women are expert at carrying around baggage loaded with guilt that really does not belong to them. We find the scriptural antidote for guilt in Hebrews: "Let us draw near to God with a sincere heart in full assurance of faith, having our hearts sprinkled to cleanse us from a guilty conscience" (Heb 10:22).

ABORTION AND GUILT

As we discussed earlier, we tend to manipulate circumstances to solve our problems—rather than trusting God to help us. Since the legalization of abortion, many women choose this option for the legalization of abortion, many women choose this option for solving the problem of an unwanted pregnancy. They see it as an easy way out of an embarrassing or inconvenient situation, and feel it gives them control over their own lives.

What they don't realize is that getting an abortion often causes feelings of extreme shame, grief, and guilt; it also makes them vulnerable to spirits of murder and suicide. When they take matters into their own hands they end up walking into strong bondage.

Kay, who lived an ungodly single lifestyle before she became a Christian, has experienced the guilt and heartache of abortion three times. After the abortions, while married to an abusive alcoholic and drug addict, she again became pregnant. This time, even though she didn't know God, she begged him for a healthy baby. She knew she didn't deserve it, but the Lord mercifully gave her a beautiful healthy daughter. A short time later Kay committed her life to Christ. She shares her story:

> Ginger was two years old when we got a divorce, and my ex-husband remarried a week later. God began dealing with my sins as I stopped focusing on my ex-husband's sins and asked the Lord to begin working in my heart.
>
> I knew that Jesus shed his blood for all my sins, including the murders of my babies; however, I also knew there was more to the healing process. I felt no remorse for these abortions—absolutely nothing. I learned that we can become callous to areas of sin and rejection in our lives, which produces the lack of feeling.
>
> One night at an all-night prayer meeting I had a vision. I saw myself standing at the foot of Jesus' cross holding my three aborted babies. They were bloody, twisted, and torn. I looked up into Jesus' face and saw such sadness and heartache as he looked at the babies and at me. A warm, peaceful flow of Jesus' blood began to flow down from the cross onto me....
>
> Though I was a sinner, I was also a victim of my own sin. He not only forgave, but exchanged the horribleness of murder

with the pure beauty of his perfect gift of love. I knew how much he loved me and how much he loved my precious daughter, Ginger. She was his gift to me even before I knew him. I wept and wept.

The stark reality was this: No matter what I knew or didn't know at the time of the abortions, I was, in fact, three times a murderer of my own flesh and blood. The babies had suffered and died because of my choices. As a mother, I desperately wanted to comfort them, and felt the deep pain of not being able to. I felt the pain, horror, and guilt of being a murderer. I couldn't cancel it or change it. I was helpless.

With my pride completely broken and a rush of cleansing tears, I received Jesus' love like never before. I surrendered my life more completely that day. I was able to share, minutely, in his suffering. How much we hurt our wonderful God when we sin!

He has truly given me beauty for ashes. The joy I have far outweighs the pain. I can now say with confidence, "I am forgiven and the shame and guilt of being a murderer is completely gone!"

Now active in anti-abortion campaigns, Kay has worked through her grief and guilt to accept God's forgiveness. Yet she still sheds many tears. "I cry for the dying, unwanted babies. I cry for the confused, love-starved mothers. I cry when I hear of other people choosing to serve the god of convenience and selfishness."[5]

THE VIRTUOUS WOMAN

What is our goal? To become the women God created us to be. One of the scriptural models of that is the virtuous woman of Proverbs 31: "She is a woman of strength and dignity, and has no fear of old age. When she speaks, her words are wise, and kindness is the rule for everything she says" (Prv 31:25-26, LB).

One translation says she is clothed with strength and dignity—

the exact opposite of the cloak of shame (mentioned at the beginning of this chapter) which Corrie wore until the Lord removed it. Strength is the capacity to sustain force without yielding or breaking; it speaks of solidity, tenacity, and a source of power. Dignity means the state or quality of being excellent, worthy, or honorable; nobility of manner.

Women filled with God's spirit are women of power—persons of strength, might, authority, and ability. We have two kinds of power: *exousia,* meaning "delegated authority," and *dunamis* (from which we get dynamite or dynamic), referring to authority on the *inside*—that which comes from the the Holy Spirit. Our Proverbs 31 example is not only strong, powerful, and valiant; she's dynamic in authority.

As you walk out of bondage, shedding your cloak of shame and guilt, you can model your walk with God after this virtuous woman. Think of yourself as a *daughter of the King*, part of a royal priesthood, and a virtuous woman with a reverential fear and love for the Lord.

As you read further, you may recognize other unholy garments you want to shed in exchange for robes of strength and dignity. You can trade grief and bitterness for joy, anger for inner peace, disappointment for hope, immmorality for purity, fear for trust.

PRAYER

Lord, I choose to let you clothe me with your robe of righteousness. But first, I relinquish to you my old, unclean garments of shame and guilt. I truly desire to be a woman of strength and dignity, empowered by your Spirit, joyful in the unique image you've created me to be. Thank you that you will help me to become a dynamic woman, walking in your love and blessing. Thank you, Lord, for taking my guilt and shame upon the cross so I no longer need to carry it. Amen.

EIGHT

Fear vs. Trust

There is no fear in love. But perfect love drives out fear, because fear has to do with punishment. The one who fears is not made perfect in love.

1 John 4:18

All kinds of fears plague women in today's world. Some of the major ones they share with us are:

- fear of being alone
- fear of the dark
- fear of abandonment
- fear of failure
- fear of disapproval or ridicule
- fear of financial lack
- fear of injury or violence
- fear of cancer or disabling sickness
- fear of suffering and pain
- fear of death
- fear of losing a loved one
- fear of losing a relationship
- fear of losing independence
- fear of the future

Fear. Dread. Alarm. Some women live in perpetual fear— especially for their children or husbands. Fear can be beneficial when it warns us of impending danger, but when taken to extremes, and coupled with worry, it quickly becomes a heavy bondage. If we Christian women allow fear to dominate our thoughts, we're really telling God we don't trust him. We don't mean to send that message, but somehow we have gotten so caught up in fearful worry, we don't realize the depth of our bondage.

LEAH HID HER FEARS

Leah is a talented young wife and mother who would impress you as really "having it together." She has a godly, supportive husband, two beautiful little girls, a lovely home, and lots of friends. Yet for much of her life she struggled desperately against paralyzing fear. Perhaps you will see yourself in some part of her story.

At about age four Leah was hospitalized with severe bronchitis, which developed into asthma. From that time on, she was in and out of hospitals with frequent asthma attacks. As she related her story, she said that somehow she picked up the idea that she would not live very long—perhaps from overhearing doctors discussing her case. She related:

> It was terrifying not to be able to breathe during these attacks, and I was afraid to die. My mother was very fearful, as was my grandmother; their overprotectiveness only reinforced my fears. Our family went to church regularly, but I tended to think of God as being fearful rather than loving.
>
> My mother worked to help pay medical bills, and she hired 'nannies' to take care of me. Most of them really loved me, and I was a fairly compliant child. But I remember some of them who would threaten, "If you don't behave I'll throw you out in the road and a car will run over you." I was terrified, because I thought they really would.

I had an uncle who, at family gatherings, would say to me, "I'm going to put you in a gunny-sack, tie it up and throw it in the river."

Maybe he did that because he delighted to see the terror on my face. My cousins ignored him because they knew he was teasing, but I believed anything an adult said. I would run and hide under the bed and refuse to come out until he had left the house. Two of these older cousins taunted me unmercifully and threatened all kinds of things. It just seemed my whole world was full of fear.

Toward the end of her ninth-grade year, Leah's life changed dramatically when she experienced the infilling of the Holy Spirit. A short time later, during a church service, her pastor felt impressed to pray against the evil spirit he believed was causing her asthma attacks (asthma is not always caused by demonic activity, but her pastor prayed this way in Leah's case). She literally felt something leave her body, and she suffered only one brief attack after that time. Still, she continued to struggle with many of her old fears.

After her marriage, when her husband had to travel, Leah began to fear that Dan might, like his own father, leave her for another woman. Every time he went on a trip she wanted minute details on what he was doing, where he was staying, who he was with. She asked questions under the guise of showing an interest in his work, but in her heart she was overwhelmed by suspicion and fear of betrayal.

I finally realized I had to be honest and tell Dan about my fears. He was oblivious to what my true feelings were. As we talked and got things out in the open, he dispelled my fears and I realized I really could trust him.

But my fear of being alone was still very much alive, even after our daughters were born. When Dan was out of town I wouldn't go to bed until I had looked in every closet and behind every shower curtain. I had to check and double-check to be absolutely sure all doors were locked and that no one was hiding in my house. Despite my exhaustion, I scarcely slept until Dan got home again.

WINNING BATTLES IN THE MIND

The turning point came late one night when, with the children sleeping and the house quiet, Leah suddenly heard one of the girls' wind-up musical toys begin to play. A fall from a shelf probably had activated the mechanism, but she was too terrified to go check. She phoned close friends and told them how frightened she was; they came to stay the night with her.

But as she prayed about the crisis, Leah finally realized this was a spiritual battle she would have to fight on her own. She couldn't depend upon Dan to intervene and make this problem go away. With his encouragment and support, she herself had to stand against the enemy's attack on her mind.

Dan helped me understand that the best defense is a good offense. If I was in a defensive mode, it was too late—the enemy already had the upper hand. I took the Scriptures as my offensive weapon, especially Psalm 91. A footnote in my Amplified Bible says, "The rich promises of this whole chapter are dependent upon one's meeting exactly the condition of these first two verses."

"He who dwells in the secret place of the Most High shall remain stable and fixed under the shadow of the Almighty (Whose power no foe can withstand). I will say of the Lord, He is my refuge and my fortress, my God, on Him I lean and rely, and in Him I (confidently) trust!" (Ps 91:1-2).

First, I had to work on truly dwelling in God and declaring, "Lord, I choose to trust you and to rely upon you." Then I began going to the places I always had to check—the front door, the closets, the shower curtain—and proclaiming aloud the promises in Psalm 91. I would thank the Lord for sending his angels to protect me and my household. Every time I felt fear rising in me, I would use the Scriptures against it.

One night I had been up late, reading and ironing. When I went to get ready for bed, I saw on the floor next to the bed a scorpion. But I was not afraid. Actually, I was angry, realizing I could easily have been stung. After putting on a pair of Dan's boots I stomped on the detestable thing and shouted, "Devil, you are defeated, in Jesus' name!" Then I picked it up and flushed it down the toilet. I knew my righteous anger was a sign that the fear was gone.

ENFORCING THE VICTORY

Soon Leah saw in her older daughter the same fearful reactions that she had experienced as a child. Becky was frightened of anyone with a slightly unusual appearance, afraid of animals, and afraid for Leah to be out of her sight. One day while visiting relatives, Leah and Becky were standing by the swimming pool. In a split second when Leah glanced away, two-year-old Becky fell in. Leah jumped in, pulled her out, and got the water out of her. But the child was hysterical with fear, and after that would not get into the tub for a bath.

"I began to understand that this was a generational thing in my family," Leah said. "I felt that I had broken it in my own life, but I knew that freak accident was the enemy testing it in Becky."

For the next two months Dan would put on his swim trunks at bath time, get in the tub, then hold Becky while Leah bathed her, kicking and screaming. Dan patiently comforted Becky, assuring her she had nothing to fear. Her father's assurances, and the fact that she had no more traumatic experiences in water, gradually helped her to overcome her fear. Today, at age seven, Becky swims and plays in the water with no problem. Leah shared:

I am careful to teach my girls the importance of caution without instilling fear. We've taught them that when they feel afraid they must say, "There's no fear, in Jesus' name." Sometimes Becky wants me to say it for her, but I insist that she must say it for herself.

We've also taught them 1 John 4:4: "Little children… greater is he that is in you, than he that is in the world" (KJV). Then we tell them, "Remember, the devil is only this big," and measure one inch with thumb and index finger, "but Jesus inside of you is this big," stretching both arms as wide as they will go. The Scripture is our greatest weapon to enforce the victory we've seen in our family.

WHERE DID THIS FEAR COME FROM?

In Leah's story, the fear that had dominated her mother and grandmother entered her during her early years. Often fears and other problems that gain a foothold in childhood continue to terrorize us throughout our adult life. Other fears seem to wait until we're adults, then out of nowhere, BAM—invade us, catching us off guard.

If you are plagued by intense fear, ask the Lord to show you the source of that fear. Perhaps you were hurt on a school playground. Or in a car accident. Maybe fear began to grip you in a hospital surgical ward, where you almost died. If you lost a parent through death or divorce when you were young, you may struggle with a fear of being abandoned. If you've lost your husband's love to another woman, fear of trusting men may be your stronghold.

I (Quin) allowed fear to grip me one morning right after my husband left for work at 5:00 A.M. As I watched him drive off I was horrified to see two men leap from behind some bushes and head for our front door. We lived in the woods with no close neighbors. One knocked and shouted, "We need to use your phone to call a wrecker. Our car is stuck in the sand down the way."

Fortunately, a college student was our houseguest at the time. He talked to them without opening the door, assuring them that he would call the wrecker but he would not allow them to come in. They finally left.

Later I learned from the police that the men had robbed a nearby convenience store, taken a hostage, and were armed and dangerous. The officer told me how "lucky" I was the armed men didn't shoot their way into our house. When he said that, fear, like an icy black hand, grabbed my heart.

Throughout the next week, as deputies searched the woods without finding the fugitives, my fear grew bigger. I made my husband get permission to carry a gun. I refused to sleep at home at night.

It was weeks before I realized I'd given in to that ugly thing. Hadn't God protected me in the first place? Yes! Hadn't he in the past kept me safe when fire had swept all around our property, and I'd walked our grounds reading Psalm 91 aloud? Yes! Hadn't he given me the gift of praying in tongues? Yes—and I had been praying in the Spirit the whole time the men were standing at my front door. Hadn't he taught me to sing and praise in time of trouble? Yes, again!

I finally shook free of that bondage to fear by taking it to God in prayer. "Lord, I give you this fear. Take it and replace it with trust in you. Whenever I'm tempted to be fearful, give me your strength to repel it."

My experience was not without lessons. I became more alert in watching for danger—alert, but not fearful. And my trust in the Lord was greatly strengthened.

Right now you may want to examine your own heart for ways you have succumbed to the enemy's attack in this area. Pray this prayer: "Lord, please show me if I have an unhealthy amount of fear—if I am indeed in bondage. Show me where it came in and how to rid myself of it. If I need help in walking through to victory, direct me to the right prayer partner or counselor. My desire is to walk free, no longer bound. Lord, I thank you in advance. Amen."

STRONGHOLDS OF FEAR

A bondage of fear can result from experiences and traumas of the past, or be transferred by an obsessively fearful parent or caregiver. For Kate, the latter was true. She was plagued by fear of rejection from others. She would cross to the other side of the street to avoid having to speak to someone for fear of embarrassment that the person wouldn't remember her.

"My mother suffered from paranoid schizophrenia and I can remember many times, especially during the Christmas season, when she kept us home from a party because of her feelings of doom," Kate said. "Learning to swim? Mom felt drowning was a 'given,' therefore she kept us from water. Fear became a part of my childhood."

Finally, as a grown woman, Kate knew she had to admit her problem to someone and get professional help. With a trusted counselor she went through a series of prayer sessions—layer by layer uncovering the strongholds of fear, distrust, hurt, a root of bitterness, and unforgiveness. She shared her steps to eventual victory:

"Identify the problem, seek help, take risks by joining a support group, explore the pain, and express the fear. Keep praising God during your healing process, and through prayer release all the bondages. Then walk in victory!"

Kate can now jump into a swimming pool and float without fear. Christmastime gets easier and easier to enjoy. She considers it a miracle that she can hold down a job as a hospital nurse, and speak before the support group she leads for other hurting women. Fear of rejection no longer plagues her.

PANIC ATTACKS

Sometimes fears can be so debilitating that the body ceases to function normally; panic attacks are an example of this kind of extreme reaction to fear. Doctors tell us twice as many women as men exhibit panic disorders, so apparently we are especially vulnerable to fear.

Crystal was prone to intense panic attacks whenever someone surprised her by coming up behind her, or touched her without warning. She would react in terror.

If her husband touched her or tried to embrace her while she was asleep, she would fight him off. She truly loved her gentle-hearted husband and wanted to respond to him as a wife should, so this was frustrating for both of them.

Intent on finding the cause of her terrifying fear, Crystal sought help from a Christian counselor. In her first session, she recalled a part of her childhood she had buried.

As a young girl, she had idolized her father, a truck driver. Between the ages of five to thirteen she had often traveled with him.

But during prayer and counseling sessions, memories of how he had used her as a lover on those long-haul trips began to surface. "Just our little secret, Honey," he'd say as he gave her special treats.

No wonder I fight off my husband, she thought to herself. She was relieved to discover the cause of her terror seizures. "I realized I had to forgive my dad, and with God's help I finally did."

At the counselor's suggestion, whenever her husband reached toward her in bed, he was to gently remind her, "Crystal, I am your husband, not your father." Previously, their marital relations had to be "planned events"—never spontaneous love. But now ten years have passed and she's had no more fear-riddled panic attacks. She and her husband continue to enjoy a normal, loving sex life.

When painful memories are not faced and healed, they greatly interfere with normal living. That's why it is crucial for you to get help if you have undergone a traumatic experience that made you vulnerable to bondage. Certified counselors and pastors are trained to help you sort out recurring nightmares or thoughts which cripple your spiritual and emotional life.

THE BONDAGE OF WORRY

In discussing fear vs. trust, we must bring up the problem of our lack of trust in God. If you don't think you have this problem, ask yourself: When was the last time you worried? Worry sends a signal that you have not placed your trust in God. And it is a bigger bondage than we want to admit. Jesus tells us to seek his kingdom first and put away worry. "Therefore I say to you, do not worry about your life, what you will eat or what you will drink; nor about your body, what you will put on. Is not life more than food and the body more than clothing?" (Mt 6:25, NKJV).

One Bible commentator says, "Worry means: 'to divide into parts.' [It] suggests a distraction, a preoccupation with things causing anxiety, stress and pressure. Jesus speaks against worry and anxiety because of the watchful care of a heavenly Father who is ever mindful of our daily needs."[1]

Paul gave the Philippians, and us, a good antidote to worry:

> Be anxious for nothing, but in everything by prayer and supplication, with thanksgiving, let your requests be made known to God; and the peace of God, which surpasses all understanding, will guard your hearts and minds through Christ Jesus. Finally, brethren, whatever things are true, whatever things are noble, whatever things are just, whatever things are pure, whatever things are lovely, whatever things are of good report, if there is any virtue and if there is anything praiseworthy—meditate on these things. **Philippians 3:6-8, NKJV**

WAIT TO WORRY

Worry, and its companion, stress, are visitors we women are prone to entertain on a daily basis. Rather than trusting the Lord with our circumstances, we take matters into our own hands. Come on, admit it. Don't we often want to "run interference," intervene, or meet needs when we see them in our family? Aren't we sometimes even guilty of offering "worry prayers"—begging God to fix things the way we want them?

I (Quin) have been prone to worry. But one day, flying over a city known for its violence where my single daughter was living, I again began to worry about her. First I prayed for her. Then I opened a Christian magazine and out of curiosity turned to an article called "Wait to Worry" by Fred Smith. It described a survey of four thousand worriers that revealed:

- 40 percent of what people worry about has already happened, so they can do nothing about it.
- Another 30 percent of what they worry about could never happen.
- 22 percent of what they worry about, if it comes, will have so little effect that it isn't worth worrying about.
- By process of elimination, only 8 percent of our worries are "worth the worry."[2]

The article's author described sitting in a hospital waiting room while his wife was undergoing surgery for a brain tumor. When he overheard one of the medical staff, who had emerged from the operating area, giving a bad report to someone else about a woman in surgery named Smith, Fred had to *choose* not to worry. After all, he didn't have any facts yet; he decided he'd wait until he had all his facts in—no rumors, no "what-ifs."

Some time later, Fred discovered there were two Smiths being operated on at the same time; the message he had overheard was for the other one, not his wife.

Looking back on the incident, Fred remembers forcing himself to fill the void that worry had occupied with positive thinking and good humor.

"More often than not, what we worry about today we often laugh about tomorrow," he writes. "Our worry is evidence of an inner insecurity. As Christians, we know where to find security.... Take your burden to the Lord, and leave it there," he advises.[3]

As you can imagine, by the time I'd finished the article my worry over my daughter had turned to praise—for God's provision for my child, for his protection, his love, his purpose for her life.

Most of us need to guard against letting worry lead us into bondage. Wait to worry! And in the waiting, learn to trust God when our fears arise. Otherwise, we will have a giant case of bondage on our hands.

SCRIPTURES TO MEDITATE UPON

When I am afraid,
  I will trust in you.
In God, whose word I praise,
  in God I trust; I will not be afraid.
What can mortal man do to me? **Psalm 56:3-4**

Trust in the Lord with all your heart
  and lean not on your own understanding;
in all your ways acknowledge him,
  and he will make your paths straight. **Proverbs 3:5-6**

But let all those who take refuge and put their
  trust in You rejoice;
  let them ever sing and shout for joy,
because You make a covering over them and defend them;
  let those also who love Your name be joyful in You and be
  in high spirits. **Psalm 5:11, Amplified**

But blessed is the man who trusts in the Lord,
  whose confidence is in him.
He will be like a tree planted by the water
  that sends out its roots by the stream.

It does not fear when heat comes;
  its leaves are always green.
It has no worries in a year of drought
  and never fails to bear fruit.

Jeremiah 17:7-8

PRAYER

Heavenly Father, I truly desire to become enmeshed in your love—the kind of love that never lets go. Then there will be no fear in my life, because your perfect love casts out my fear. Thank you, Lord, for increasing my understanding of your unconditional love. Help me to walk in it every day, and to show your love to others. Help me to set aside worry and replace it with trust. I ask in Jesus' name. Amen.

NINE

Family Ties That Bind

You shall not worship them [idols] or serve them; for I, the Lord your God, am a jealous God, visiting the iniquity of the fathers on the children, and on the third and the fourth generations of those who hate Me, but showing lovingkindness to thousands, to those who love Me and keep My commandments.

Deuteronomy 5:9-10, NASB

"Some family trees grow heart disease!" a sign in the doctor's office announced. I (Quin) was waiting for the nurse to give me a flu shot. As much as I hate immunizations, I prefer a shot to catching a disease that could land me in bed. "Good preventive medicine," the doctor had urged.

The medical world has produced clear evidence that heredity is a factor in the diagnosis of medical problems—everything from heart disease to cancer to obesity. Most doctors consider getting a patient's family medical history a critical part of an accurate diagnosis. During a routine physical, a skillful doctor, armed with this information, can recommend preventive measures to help you ward off ill health that may have plagued your grandparents.

Theresa's father was one of seven children—a family with six males. Five of the men had either died of heart attacks or faced multiple bypass heart surgeries. Her dad had died of the same disease that had killed his mother—Alzheimer's.

I asked Theresa, an experienced professional counselor, what her family might have done differently to protect their health.

> First, they could have changed their diet and eaten foods that were lower in fat, thus keeping their cholesterol and their weight under control.
>
> Second, they could have controlled their emotions better. They were all worriers—worried about little stuff that didn't really matter—and they verbalized their worries all the time.
>
> Third, they could have sought the Lord's help in breaking the propensity for heart disease in their family line, if they'd had the spiritual understanding to do so.

As Christians, we must acknowledge that some of the problems we experience are due to our own disobedience to God and his Word. And yet our spiritual heritage also influences the events of our lives, both positively and negatively.

In this chapter, we will explore patterns of behavior attributable to our ancestral line, and suggest solutions and preventive measures.

FACING GENERATIONAL SIN

In the verses quoted at the beginning of this chapter, God declares that he visits the iniquity of the fathers upon the children to the third and fourth generations of those who hate him. "But that's Old Testament," you may say. "Doesn't the New Testament say we are new creatures in Christ when we come to know Christ in a personal way?" Yes, we are new creatures in him, but we bring a lot of garbage with us that needs to be dumped.

The iniquity of the forefathers brings a curse upon the family line. This word iniquity does not mean individual sinful acts; it means "perverseness" and comes from a Hebrew root meaning "to be bent or crooked."[1] The word implies a basic attitude of rebellion, plus the consequences that iniquity produces. We see the same word in the prophecy concerning Jesus the Messiah: "The Lord has laid on him the iniquity of us all" (Is 53:6b). Jesus bore the cumulative sinfulness of mankind.

We are not responsible for our forefathers' individual acts of sin; we *are* responsible for plenty of our own. Galatians 3:13 declares that Jesus became a curse for us, providing a means for our deliverance. Yet we inherit a susceptibility to sin in the same areas that troubled our forefathers. We tend to be "bent or crooked" in the same places. Our enemy knows where our weak areas are because his agents have been working against our family members for generations.[2]

Author Catherine Marshall calls this "the law of generational weakness." Long after she was a mature Christian, she recognized that her own problem with fear was rooted in experiences with her Grandmother Sarah, who had been her childhood caretaker for several months when she was twelve. She writes about it in her book *Something More:*

> At this impressionable time of my life, I somehow focused on Grandmother's fears... things which seemed to me ludicrous and absurd. Such phobias were the last things I wanted to imitate.
>
> Yet so strong is the Law of the Generations that even what we scorn can still come down to us. In my case it was not Grandmother Sarah's particular fears—rather simply an over-inclination to fear. In my life it centered on a dread of germs and illness; a horror of mice and small dead animals, and during my childhood, fear of the dark, ghosts, and the like.
>
> The time came when I realized that in Jesus' eyes, fear is a sin since it is acting out a lack of trust in God.[3]

What did Catherine do about it? First, she acknowledged the truth stated in Exodus 20:5 and Deuteronomy 5:9 (quoted at the beginning of this chapter), which she had always wondered about:

> Now in the light of the revelation about my fear and Grandmother Sarah, I saw that the Exodus verse was simply stating a fact of life. And I was the third generation from my grandmother to be beset by those petty fears.
>
> ... We are accustomed to the idea that we pass on to our children a physical inheritance—color of eyes, color of hair, even certain diseases.... Handing down a material inheritance is such standard practice that the laws of every country make careful provisions governing wills, probate, death and inheritance taxes. I began to ask myself, is it possible that our spiritual inheritance is as real as the others?
>
> It soon became apparent that just as we can inherit either a fortune or debts, so in the spiritual realm we can inherit either spiritual blessings or those liabilities (unabashedly called "sins" in Scripture) that hinder our development into mature persons.[4]

When Catherine desired to break the bondage of fear, or any other sinister pattern in her family line, she and her only son Peter prayed together. She shares how their "prayer work" fell into three parts:

> First, having brought into the light all remembered dark heritage from previous generations, I had to forgive all these ancestors and release them from my judgment.
>
> Second, Peter prayed that I be cut loose from these negatives. As I remember it, his prayer went something like this:
>
> > Lord Jesus, You came to earth to loose all bonds, to set every captive free. Lord, Mother has been captive to these fears that we've been laying out before You. Yet You've declared

> that where the Spirit of the Lord is, there is liberty. So now, Lord, I take that Word and claiming it and wielding it as the Sword of the Spirit that it is, in Your Name and by Your power I hereby cut Mother free from every chain and shackle from the past. I release her now to her rightful heritage....

This powerful prayer led naturally into the third step, praising God for every part of the experience. For we found that the release would not be final unless I received it in faith, and as I had been discovering, praise is the swiftest, surest route to faith.[5]

SIN PATTERNS IN FAMILIES

Evie had been molested as a child. So had her father. Her own daughter was "date raped" at eighteen. When Evie became a Christian and realized she could do something about breaking this pattern, she sought the help of a Christian counselor. Through prayer she forgave her aggressor, and the young man who had raped her daughter. Then, realizing she had purposely gained weight to keep from being attractive to men—even to her husband—she lost forty pounds in six months.

"I told my children about the molestation pattern so they could break the bondage in our family line," she said. "Their own children wouldn't have that passed on to them. For the first time in my life, I began to like myself and to feel OK about looking good, dressing nicely, and receiving compliments. I even enjoy our marriage bed now."

We see certain sin patterns in families, even in the Bible. Abraham, for example, lied about his wife Sarah, calling her his sister *on two occasions*. Later, Abraham's son Isaac lied about his wife Rebekah, saying she was his sister. Isaac's son Jacob deceived his father in order to receive the firstborn blessing due his older brother, Esau. Jacob's sons deceived him about his son, Joseph, causing him to grieve for years.

The tendency to lie and deceive showed up in succeeding generations, each time causing more serious consequences. However, the blessings of Abraham far outweighed the bent toward sin. Praise God for that!

We see this principle at work in King David's life, too. His sin of adultery with Bathsheba showed up in sexual sin through his sons. Finally, because his son Solomon took hundreds of foreign wives and began to worship their false gods, God took the kingdom from him. The gravity of Solomon's sin was greater than that of his father David.

HAUNTING HIDDEN SECRETS

Not every problem, habit, or character trait should be blamed on generational inheritance. We activate the tendency in our generational line when we choose to sin.

When Joy discovered she was pregnant and quickly married her baby's father before anyone else suspected her condition, they both thought they had covered up "their little secret."

Then, years later, two of their three daughters also became pregnant before marriage. One placed her baby for adoption. The second had her baby and later married the child's father.

When Joy and her husband became Christians they recognized the sin pattern in their family. So they asked God to forgive them, and to forgive their daughters. They then took authority over fornication, lust, and other sexual sins that had prevailed in their family, declaring them null and void in the name and power of Jesus Christ.

When their third daughter entered her teenage years, Joy talked with her daughter openly, using the unhappy experiences of herself and her older daughters to emphasize the importance of sexual purity. Thankfully, Joy reports that her youngest took the message to heart.

This is not to imply that every problem, habit, or character trait is to be blamed on generational inheritance. Because we *choose* to sin, we activate the tendency in our generational line. Also, emotional and behavioral problems sometimes have a physiological or biological base. But if you recognize a family weakness, ask the Lord for revelation and guidance on how to address it. Confess and repent for your own sin, then educate your children so they become alert to the areas where the enemy will seek to tempt them.

GAINING FREEDOM FROM COMPULSIVE-ADDICTIVE BEHAVIOR

Let's look at what another woman did when she recognized in herself behavior characteristics similar to those of her parents. She saw the same propensity to sin in herself.

Ruth's father owned a successful business, but he was a workaholic and never came home at the time he promised he would. Her mother, who had grown up in a family of screamers, had determined when she married to keep peace at all costs—she never expressed her feelings, except to cry a lot. She had several nervous breakdowns, and three times tried to commit suicide.

"Though I didn't recognize it, I had this deep-seated need to be loved and cherished, which my parents seemed unable to meet because of their own problems," Ruth said. "I tried to be a perfect person and have my parents see me as the best girl anywhere. I'd strive for all A's in my classes and be the best athlete in any sports I participated in. I was performance-oriented, just like Mom.

"My need to be loved drove me to become sexually active at age sixteen. But multiple sexual partners couldn't fill the void in my life. Soon I began to realize how dangerous *that* was, decided to be more selective—and would only go to bed with my current boyfriend, whoever that happened to be. But when that boy jilted me, I was devastated."

Ruth had known the Lord since childhood; whenever she had

sex with her boyfriends she felt shame afterward. When she thought she'd found the perfect sex partner, she married him, but it wasn't long before he was abusing her—both verbally and sexually. After seven years of marriage he deserted her and their two small children.

She made a commitment to follow the Lord, but even then could not seem to abstain from sleeping with three different men. Next, she found herself doing what her dad had always done: becoming a workaholic. Starting on the bottom rung of the ladder in a cosmetics firm, she rose all the way to sales director, earning three new car bonuses. Working, working, working. Spending, spending, spending.

"Then the Lord allowed me to fall," she remembers. "My business fell. I came face-to-face with the term 'compulsive-addictive behavior.' I realized I had a personality disorder just like my dad. Without consciously being aware of it, I had bought into the idea of wanting to be like him."

GAINING FREEDOM

Ruth hit rock bottom emotionally and cried out to the Lord for help. She remembers telling God she wanted to bring her addictions under control—sex, shopping, perfectionism, and workaholic tendencies. She went to a counselor for help, but it was mostly by learning to talk with the Lord that she gained freedom. In her own words, here's what she did to get free:

1. I faced my own sin and asked God to forgive me. Yes, I had had a lousy marriage. Yes, everybody I trusted had walked out on me. Yes, I could blame others, but I had to face my own sin and ask God's forgiveness.
2. I had to forgive myself. This proved to be a process as memories turned up things I thought I could never forgive myself for. With each memory I'd stop and say, "Jesus, please forgive me. I receive your forgiveness, and now I choose to forgive myself."

3. I had to change what I thought about myself, and speak out what God thinks about me. I had associated words with myself like "slut, failure, compulsive spender, performer," and I had to realign my thinking. I began to read the Bible fervently, and for five years collected and memorized Scriptures that declare who I am in Christ—loved and accepted in the Beloved—and I'd repeat them.
4. I had a fear that I'd fall again into the same sin pattern. I was also afraid of night noises. Whenever fear showed its ugly head—which was often at night—I'd wake up and read Scriptures that say "fear not." One night I read the entire book of Deuteronomy underlining the *fear nots*. I was never afraid again.
5. I recognized that God was never going to walk out on me as other people had. I could count on him to cut generational sin because I asked him to.
6. When my mom and I discovered that some relatives in my family's past had also had premarital sex, I realized my own rebellion as a sixteen-year-old in love with an older man may have been related to generational sin. Mom and I prayed together and broke the tendency toward this iniquity in me, and asked God to remove it from my children's lives.
7. I knew the generational sin was broken in my family when I made a less-than-perfect grade in my college class recently. My son repeated to me what I'd said to him once, "Mom, God doesn't care what our grades are; God cares that we tried." My children are no longer performers and neither am I. My daughter used to cry if her room wasn't perfect, but no more.

As a result of her efforts, Ruth now reports, "I've lived a celibate life for nine years now. And I no longer have the need to buy, buy, buy. I bought a house and decorated it in a feminine Victorian style—showing the new me. I have a business in my home and I'm attending college to get my degree to be a counselor. My wounded self-esteem has been healed—by the help of the Lord."

Maybe you can identify with some of the compulsive behavior

in Ruth's life. She recognized tendencies in herself from both her parents—the workaholic from her dad, the perfectionism from her mom. Years before she discovered this release of her spirit, Ruth had even tried to commit suicide, just as her mom had. But now Ruth tells her children that those sin patterns do not need to show up in their lives, as long as they walk in obedience to the Lord.

ALCOHOLICS AND THEIR CHILDREN

Drs. David and Sharon Sneed, in their book *Understanding Your Family Chemistry*, tell us that alcoholism does run in families. They report studies done by others:

> First-degree relatives of alcoholics—which includes daughters, sons, and parents, or what we commonly call the nuclear family—are up to seven times as likely as other people to become alcoholics themselves.
>
> The most compelling evidence linking genetics with the transmission of alcoholism comes from studies of adopted children and their biological parents. These studies eliminate most environmental facts that might otherwise shroud the association between biological inheritance and alcohol abuse. Indeed, such tests indicate an adopted child with at least one biological parent who was alcoholic is two-and-a-half times more likely to develop alcoholism—regardless of the environmental situation with his adoptive parents or the degree of exposure to the alcoholic parent.[6]

My friend Sonya is a case in point. So far she has lived to see three generations of alcoholics in her family line; in her research she has uncovered many other such cases.

Sonya's abusive alcoholic father died in a mental hospital. When she was barely out of her teens she fell in love and married an alcoholic who wanted to control her and expected her to join him on his drinking binges. Her husband was an outfitter-guide who prided himself on taking hunters into the wilds to get the best elk or deer trophy ever. He also provided hunters with wild drinking parties and women. He himself was having extramarital affairs.

Sonya tried to be a good mother to their four daughters, but she also drank a lot and found herself becoming suicidal. She kept a pistol hidden away for the day when she could plan her own death. Knowing she needed help she turned to God, the church, and an organization for recovering alcoholics. Finally she checked into a treatment center for codependents in another state.

When she went to see her children after she was released from the treatment center, her husband fought to keep them away from her. He also turned her friends against her with lies and accusations. Finally, he filed for divorce and won custody of the girls—despite the fact that he had a live-in, alcoholic girlfriend for the next seven years.

Sonya returned to the city where she'd gotten treatment; Christian friends there gave her prayer support. There she found work and started her life over again.

Today her daughters are ages 20, 17, 15, and 14, and they spend their weekends drinking. "The oldest buys a case of beer every Friday night for them and they cruise around and get drunk," Sonya said. "They live with their dad and work for him driving wagon trains—they love the horses. But he's turned them against me. I pray someday they will know how much I love them."

Despite the heartache of being separated from her girls, unable to intervene as they make choices that she knows will bring them grief, Sonya is thankful for her own newfound freedom. She recounts for us the steps of her healing process:

1. I turned to God and admitted my problem, and my need for help.
2. I checked into the treatment center because for me I needed that help and counsel—but not every alcoholic or codependent needs a treatment center.
3. I surrounded myself with a support system—mainly Christian friends—to whom I was accountable. This way I have stayed free of alcohol all these years.

4. I had to keep forgiving my husband—and it is a process. It is painful not to see my children on their birthdays or holidays. But at least I have been cut free from my husband's abuse.
5. I do volunteer work and reach out to others, which keeps me from being too self-centered.

"Now after eight years, I think I am ready for a Christian boyfriend who will respect me. I am no longer in bondage to fear of the past."

Drs. David and Sharon Sneed again remind us:

> Genetic predisposition is an important factor, but it is not all-powerful. You don't have to be an alcoholic just because your mother or father was an alcoholic.... Think prevention. Prevent alcoholism, drug addiction, and obesity from occurring rather than trying to mop up after it has become a reality. This should certainly be our focus for the next generation of predisposed addicts.[7]

Nehemiah identified with the sin of his family. He was an exiled Jew in Babylon, cupbearer to the King of Persia, when he learned that the walls of Jerusalem, home of his ancestors, lay in ruins. He wept, mourned, fasted, and prayed because of the condition of his homeland (a good example for any intercessor). "I confess the sins we Israelites, including myself and my father's house, have committed against you. We have acted very wickedly toward you. We have not obeyed the commands, decrees and laws you gave your servant Moses" (Neh 1:6b-7).

Confessing the iniquities of our ancestors and family members, as Nehemiah did, is an effective way to break patterns of generational sin. Daniel too confessed the sins of his ancestors when he called upon the Lord in prayer. Read it in Daniel 9:3, 5, 11, 17-19.

PRAYER TO BREAK GENERATIONAL PATTERNS

Lord Jesus Christ, I believe that you are the Son of God and that you redeemed us from the curse of the law by becoming a curse for us as is written in Galatians 3:13.

Father God, I am bold to ask for your mercy. Forgive the sin that's been in our family for generations. I ask you to blot out any sins committed by me or my ancestors that exposed us to a curse or were an abomination to you. (Then name them: adultery, occult involvement of any kind, substance abuse, stealing, murder, rebellion, idolatry, and any others the Lord shows you as you read Deuteronomy 27, 28, 30.)

Lord, I repent and ask that you take these sins from my family once and for all, in the name of Jesus Christ. Father, I now receive your forgiveness and rejoice in your provision. I thank you for the blessings that have come from my ancestry, for talents and gifts and graces. Help me to fulfill your purposes for me in my generation. In Jesus' name I ask this. Amen.

Now declare to Satan and his emissaries:

I proclaim that my family is under the blood of Jesus. As a child of God, I have revoked and broken every demonic power in my life. By the blood of Jesus I stop all generational curses, and declare that ours is a generation that will serve God, and our household is holy ground.

Satan, I renounce you and all your works in my life and the life of my family. By an act of my will I close the door to you, and you have no right to harrass this family, in the name of Jesus.

Lord, please loose the supernatural power of the Holy Spirit to hover over our family and protect us from the Evil One. I give you praise in Jesus' name. Amen.

TEN

The Bondage of Addictions

Don't you know that when you offer yourselves to someone to obey him as slaves, you are slaves to the one whom you obey—whether you are slaves to sin, which leads to death, or to obedience, which leads to righteousness? **Romans 6:16**

Every weekday morning from eight until noon Deb exercised at the health club, working out on the body-building machines, doing aerobics, playing racquetball, or swimming. Then she'd go home and take a long nap before preparing supper for her husband, frequently meeting her brother-in-law for another game of racquetball afterward.

"I felt good about myself because I was working on improving my body," she said. "When I taught aerobics I felt even better because I was helping other women."

"So... is anything wrong with that?" you may ask.

Of course physical exercise itself is not wrong or sinful. But what started out as a good thing became a problem for Deb; her exercise routine began to control her, instead of the other way around. She actually became addicted to exercise.

"Finally, one day I woke up and realized I was terribly self-indulgent, and my life was controlled by my exercise program," Deb confesses.

WHAT IS ADDICTION?

A dictionary defines addiction as "given over to a pursuit, practice or habit, as addicted to drugs. Addiction suggests a pathological weakness." Akin to that is compulsion, "an irresistible impulse to perform an irrational act."

So we can say an addiction is a controlling need or desire for a substance, object, or behavior because it gives you a gratifying reaction. It can relax, excite, or satisfy you, although you would deny that it controls you. "I can stop anytime I want," you tell yourself.

The truth is, addictions are an escape mechanism. The urge to eat when you're hungry and drink when you're thirsty are normal physiological responses. But satisfying an addiction removes you from your true feelings of sadness, inadequacy, anger, or pain. First, you get into a habit of behavior or substance use, then you keep giving in to the compulsion more and more often. Soon you are dangerously hooked in an addictive bondage.

We are all familiar with some obvious addictions: to food, alcohol, drugs, shopping, work, romance novels, exercise, sex, and even religious activities.

But what about women who collect things compulsively? Like one woman I know, who never misses a Saturday morning garage sale or antique auction. Or another, who just must have that porcelain angel to add to her huge collection—even though she can't afford it. Or the woman who absolutely won't miss her three-times-a-week bridge game?

Addictions? Hardly, you say. But think about it. Whatever thing or activity that controls your thoughts and actions—that you "worship," so to speak—can easily become your bondage. No Christian woman would want to admit it, but if her hobby or collection or activity has that strong a grip on her life, she has made it an idol as surely as the children of Israel made a golden calf to worship in the wilderness. It's spiritual idolatry, plain and simple.

But we generally think of real addictions as alcohol and drugs, right? These are especially dangerous because they give the devil an open door to come in and walk around in your mind. A person addicted to drugs or alcohol becomes physiologically dependent upon the substance, while the dependency from other types of addictions is psychological and emotional. But all have spiritual roots and consequences.

Why do we get started with an addiction? For a variety of reasons: an attempt to escape worry and anxiety; a means of reducing guilt feelings; an effort to avoid pain, confusion, failure, or imperfection.

ADDICTED TO PERFECTIONISM

Cathy set for herself a daily routine so demanding it kept her in perpetual motion. To keep her body in perfect shape, she worked out two or three hours a day. Then she volunteered for numerous church activities— "serving God" was high on her priority list. After her daughter was born, Cathy resolved to be the "perfect mother." She also wanted to be a perfect wife for her husband, although most of the time he got only the dregs after her cup of energy was drained.

After sliding into a pit of postpartum depression, Cathy sought help. In therapy she faced some painful realities from her past which she had tried to block out.

First, she acknowledged that her affluent parents, who had given her everything money could buy as she was growing up, had failed to provide what she needed most: emotional bonding and nurturing.

From early childhood she had observed her father working out at a furious pace. Hoping to win his acceptance, Cathy began a rigorous exercise routine too. Her father frequently "checked her body" to make sure she was in good shape, but she never measured up. Both parents constantly criticized her, trying to motivate her to match her brother's achievements. Greatly lacking any self-confidence, she became involved in drugs and sex in her teenage years.

She recognized that her roller-coaster life of drug abuse, abortion, and a failed marriage to an abuser were the fruit of those bitter seeds of rejection planted in her childhood. Now that Cathy was serving the Lord and he had blessed her with a Christian husband and a healthy baby, she was loaded with guilt—yet still a slave to perfectionism. Her moods would swing from feelings of gratitude for her baby, to feelings of resentment that her highly organized routine was interrupted by the needs of a helpless infant.

Overwhelmed by her painful past and the compulsion to "measure up" to her standard of perfection, Cathy dropped out of therapy and went back to using drugs, prescription drugs this time. Taking diet pills and antidepressants not only helped her maintain her "perfect body" and avoid gaining weight, it spiked her energy level to help her keep up her frenetic pace. But eventually she crashed and again sought help.

WHAT IS THE ANSWER?

Addictive behavior is merely a symptom, a coping device that the addict uses to mask the pain of a deeper problem. How do women like Deb (in our opening story) and Cathy find freedom from their compulsive behavior?

Finding balance was Deb's answer. She stopped teaching aerobics and cut down on her time at the gym. Sometimes she will ride her bike or take a walk with a friend for exercise—enjoying God's creation along the way. She resists compulsion and chooses moderation.

Deb's suggestions for getting out of the exercise trap: Ask yourself, "Why am I so driven to exercise?" Is it for compliments? For self-satisfaction? For health's sake? Try to determine your underlying motivation. Then ask God to show you a more healthy approach.

In Cathy's case, a Christian counselor helped her see that her compulsive behavior stemmed from foundational unresolved issues in her life. Then she clarified for Cathy these four things which needed to happen before she could break free from her bondage:

1. She had to confess, "My life is out of control," and acknowledge that she needed help—a very painful step for someone who prided herself on organizing her life and excelling at everything.
2. She had to agree to become accountable to her husband and a friend for her behavior.
3. She had to acknowledge that she was angry with herself because no matter how hard she tried, she couldn't be perfect. She was finally able to acknowledge her imperfections and self-hatred and accept herself.
4. She had to face the pain of her father's rejection, forgive him, and begin to deal with the emotions she had stifled for so long with her addictions.

A recovered drug addict once said, "I've learned that the thing I depend upon in my life controls my life; therefore I must depend on Jesus Christ." As Cathy learned to depend upon the Lord and allow him to heal the rejection in her life, she discovered she was no longer controlled by her addictions.

The steps Deb and Cathy took in coming out of bondage will benefit any woman seeking freedom. The major keys are depending on the Lord to help you, and being accountable to someone who can encourage you, pray with you—and correct you when necessary!

IN BONDAGE TO FOOD

According to Dr. Archibald Hart, addiction to food is similar to addictions to drugs, alcohol, or other such substances. He distinguishes between enjoying food and being addicted to food, and between the food disorders called anorexia and bulimia, which keep many women in bondage:

> Anorexia is characterized by a refusal to eat sufficient food while bulimia is episodic binge eating, usually while depressed, accompanied by a fear of not being able to stop eating. After the binge, the victim induces vomiting or takes laxatives to get rid of the food.
>
> ... In both anorexia and bulimia, food itself is not the primary problem. While there is a fascination with food, the preoccupation is with avoiding it. The person may feel out of control as far as food is concerned, but it is the underlying emotional disturbance that is the real problem, not the avoiding or eating of the food....
>
> Therapy with bulimics can be extremely frustrating because they often want to focus only on the eating problem and resist facing the underlying emotional turmoil. It is these underlying problems that must be addressed in therapy. The eating problem will take care of itself when the underlying causes of self-hatred, shame, depression, and resentment have been resolved.[1]

SELF-CONSCIOUS PERFECTIONIST

Let's look at one young woman's struggle with a bondage to a food disorder. Chances are you know someone like her. Renee, a petite size four, is so friendly and outgoing she recently won her company's "friendliest employee" award. Five years ago she was a 165-pound, matronly looking college graduate, withdrawn and unsociable. For eight years Renee had struggled with bulimia.

Because her mother always seemed to be struggling with a

weight problem, Renee quickly became self-conscious about her own body image when she reached puberty. Expressions of affection were rare in her family; this enforced her feeling that being accepted was based solely on her appearance and performance.

One day in seventh grade band practice, she looked down at her thighs and said to herself, "I am fat." She scooted to the edge of her seat so her thighs wouldn't look so big. "That's when I began to believe a lie about myself," she says.

Renee became a secret eater, snacking on ice cream, candy, doughnuts, or pizza in addition to eating several meals a day. When she went to college she figured out how to use her meal ticket to eat at one dorm, then go to another and eat again. She would swallow up to thirty laxative tablets a day to get the food out of her system.

"Basically I was a perfectionist and a people-pleaser—a vicious trap, because I never felt 'good enough' to win the approval of other people. When I ate a lot I was rewarding myself, but avoiding my real problem. Eating was the only thing I thought I could control. I knew the calorie count of most foods, and I knew how to time my laxatives after eating to rid myself of what I'd just eaten. After a while the laxatives didn't work and my weight ballooned out of control. I wanted to go out with guys but I was afraid to, so in that way my weight protected me."

At home during the summers, Renee went on excessive exercise programs—tennis, running, workouts—to prove to herself and her parents that she could lose weight. But back at school, she'd begin to binge and purge again.

After eight years of fighting bulimia and its accompanying depression, she checked herself into a Christian treatment center for five weeks. There she discovered the reasons for overeating, and became accountable to someone so she didn't have to face the problem alone. She was admonished not to be so obsessed with her weight. She had to face the fact that no one is perfect.

"I had wanted the perfect figure, the perfect personality, the perfect everything!" she said. "Eating had been my selfish pastime.

At the Christian counseling center, I learned to accept myself as God made me. I had to take responsibility for my own choices, and stop blaming my parents—or anyone else—for the disappointments in my life."

While in counseling she learned biblical principles, concentrated on the Word of God, and clung to this verse as her lifeline:

> No temptation has overtaken you except such as is common to man; but God is faithful, who will not allow you to be tempted beyond what you are able, but with the temptation will also make the way of escape, that you may be able to bear it.
>
> **1 Corinthians 10:13, NKJV**

Over and over she prayed, "Lord, provide the way of escape when I am tempted to overeat." And God has helped her during the past five years to eat moderately and to follow a reasonable exercise routine. Also, she does a lot of walking on her job.

Renee has accepted the reality that she will make mistakes, but she's not anxious about it. She's also learned to stop the hateful self-talk, such as, "You're so stupid—why did you do that again?" Or, "I'm always a loser!"

This woman's acceptance of herself—imperfections and all—is essential to her developing a healthy self-image and staying out of bondage.

"SHOP 'TIL YOU DROP"

Have you ever thought about being addicted to shopping—an insatiable desire for new clothes, for instance? Or maybe you are a grandmother who overbuys for grandchildren. You just can't seem to resist the urge.

Some women confess that when they're nervous or depressed, shopping is their favorite panacea. The average woman carries ten credit cards in her purse. And the majority of advertising is directed toward women, because merchandisers know that women do most of the shopping.

"Born to shop." "A woman's place is in the mall." You've seen these bumper stickers on cars. And you've probably laughed at them. But shopping is a real bondage to some women.

Shortly after Christmas the *Dallas Morning News* carried an article entitled, "Shopping Addicts Buying Trouble."

Dr. Irving Kolin, a Florida psychiatrist specializing in addiction, said,

> Compulsive shopping has to be seen as a symptom of a problem rather than a problem itself. Many needs can be fulfilled with shopping. For those who are feeling isolated, the interaction with salespeople is often a social thing. Overspending can be a passive-aggressive way for a person to express anger with a spouse. Shopping also is used to combat low self-esteem, depression and any other number of problems common to those with addictions.[2]

One reader told us she was so obsessed with controlling and spending money that she had stooped to stealing from members of her family. Her husband opened a separate checking account in his name only, but she stole blank checks from his wallet and forged his signature. "I hated myself for what I was doing to my family," she said, "but I had lost control of myself in this area." She felt her bondage was so hopeless that she prayed to die, and contemplated suicide.

At the beauty shop one day she bought a copy of our book *A Woman's Guide to Spiritual Warfare*. Staying up most of the night to read, she recognized herself in the book's pages and cried out to God for help. She renounced her addiction, rededicated her life to the Lord, and asked him to fill her with the Holy Spirit. She confessed to her husband and children, and returned a check she had stolen. "I feel like a changed person," she said exuberantly. "I'm free at last—I know life will be different for me now."

ADDICTED BARGAIN HUNTER

Francine was so obsessed with bargain hunting that for years she spent most of her office lunch breaks window shopping instead of eating. On weekends she generally went "mall-hopping" in search of bargains. But when she quit her job and her husband neared retirement Francine realized she truly was addicted, and she began seeking God's help.

"For many people with this problem, getting free is a gradual thing," she reports. "You have to break the old habit of buying compulsively, and with God's help learn to weigh each purchase carefully."

To stay out of bondage, Francine follows these guidelines:

1. Before going shopping I ask God to help me avoid temptation, and to be a wise and prudent shopper.
2. I determine in advance that I will do ***no impulse buying***, but stick to what's on my shopping list or within my specified budget. I choose ***not*** to buy something I really don't need just because it's a bargain.
3. I don't spend whole days "window shopping" lest I be tempted to buy. Instead, I spend more time with Christian friends and in ministry activities that count for the Lord.

BREAKING FROM "ADDICTION BUILDUP"

Dr. Archibald Hart has succinctly captured the essence of addictions:

> Because the basic drive in addiction is to avoid painful feelings and experiences, anything that masks these feelings can become an "addictive" cover or escape. Over time, the addictive behavior becomes less effective at blocking the feelings we want to avoid—so we have to ingest the substance or practice the behavior again and again, more and more often, in order to

achieve the desired effect.... It is here that the potential for sin is very great.[3]

In addition to the negative effects of addictions, this "potential for sin" is the reason addictive behavior is a serious spiritual issue. Drug addictions plague even Christian women, whether they live in cities or small-town America.

Marilyn was not a Christian when she started smoking marijuana as a teen. She soon switched to street drugs: speed, LSD, and eventually, cocaine. When she got pregnant in high school, she stopped taking drugs temporarily. As soon as her baby's father got out of jail she married him, hoping to help him kick his drug habit.

By the time she was twenty-one, Marilyn had two babies and held down three jobs. She still took drugs occasionally, especially at parties, but she didn't think she was addicted. One day after a pastor invited her to church, she and her husband made a public commitment to follow Jesus.

But Marilyn's husband was soon back into the drug culture, and overdosed on several occasions. Friends would drop him off at her front door, fearing he was dead, and she'd pump his chest to get him breathing again.

"I was still trying to follow God, even though my husband wouldn't," she reported. "I began crying out, 'God, please save my husband—please change him. He's unfaithful and doing drugs—this is no way for a husband and father to act. Lord, I've given you everything—my life, my sons, all I have—and I want you to save my husband. Answer me!'"

Despite her desperate prayers, her husband's behavior grew worse. When his adultery and drug and alcohol abuse became more than she could bear, Marilyn pursued a double divorce: from her husband—and from God.

"One night in a fit of anger I cried out, 'God, I divorce you! You didn't answer my prayer for my husband—you didn't save him like I prayed—I divorce you. You no longer have permission to work in my life.'

"It was one of the most horrible mistakes I've ever made. What I didn't realize was that I was giving Satan a foothold in my life. I have learned that if you don't serve God, you serve his enemy—Satan and all his demonic kingdom. I not only returned to drugs, I began 'free-basing' cocaine. Within a few months I married a dirty old man who was into pornography and alcohol."

Marilyn ended up in a rehabilitation hospital, and her husband walked out on her. Her life continued to go downhill: more drug abuse, hospitalizations in a psychiatric unit, and two suicide attempts—once by a drug overdose, the second time by slashing her wrists.

"In divorcing God I had released spirits into my life—especially spirits of suicide," she related. "Finally my brother, a pastor, took me and my sons in, providing housing and lots of Christian counseling and love." Under her brother's discipline, and surrounded by the love and prayers of his congregation, Marilyn determined to change. She attended Bible school for a year to get grounded in the Word of God.

"It was so important to renew my mind with the Word—to bathe myself in God's promises and know that he accepted me, a lost lamb, back into the fold," she said. "I went on a fast, and during that time I remember experiencing deep repentance—and incredible joy."

Then she addressed the enemy: "Satan, I release myself from your hold. You can no longer have me. You are God's enemy and my enemy and I place you under my feet. You will no longer steal my life."

After her declaration she prayed, "God, I allow you to be my Daddy—my God. I love you. I will serve you forever."

Following that victory she went to visit Christian relatives over Thanksgiving. But the enemy was not finished harassing or tormenting her. "You aren't worthy—why don't you kill yourself so your sons can live with these wonderful relatives and have a decent home for a change?" the voice taunted her. "They can give the boys everything you can't." Over and over the words played in her mind

Marilyn fell for the deception and slit her wrists in another unsuccessful suicide attempt. By now most of her relatives were so disappointed in her, they had little hope—or answers. They sent her to live with her mother (who was deaf), where she recuperated, then got a job as a waitress. While at her mother's home, a Christian man kept coming there to learn sign language.

"Scott and I developed a friendship, and though he had never done drugs and had much more education than I did, he appreciated my honesty about my past. He accepted me just as I was. Within two years we were married. Now, eight years later, we have a solid Christian marriage, and we've been able to help my two sons find counseling for their drug problems."

Remember, the enemy will test your deliverance. Marilyn has been free of drugs for some years now, but she realizes she must choose to remain free.

"For me, it will be a lifetime of depending upon God," she said. "I walk daily with the Lord, asking him not to let me fall. I say every day, 'I choose life, not death. I choose God, not the devil's lies.' My husband keeps the medication I take for a chronic condition and gives it to me when I need it. This makes me accountable to him, and it's a safeguard against temptation.

"I could transfer my drug addiction to other things, like food, over-the-counter pills, or wine. Sometimes I still struggle with depression. One evening during the Christmas season my depression came back, but Scott took authority over those tormenting spirits and demanded that they release me. Within half an hour I was free, and we had a wonderful Christmas together."

SPIRITUAL IDOLATRY

In reviewing stories of the women in this chapter we see a common thread running through them. In each case the woman gradually fell into an unwholesome habit of behavior, which over time became an addiction. She became enslaved to that sin when satisfying the addiction took preeminence over everything, even the Lord.

We need to remember that addictions have spiritual connotations. Our human nature is basically rebellious and self-centered. Addictions are, to put it bluntly, spiritual idolatry. Addictions keep us depending on things to satisfy us, rather than relying on a loving God.

Augustine once said, "Idolatry is worshiping anything that ought to be used, or using anything that ought to be worshiped."

What a warning! As Christians you and I must not place our affections on things that enslave us. The Holy Spirit can help us begin to recognize early signs of addictive bondages.

Maybe you feel you've sunk too far—perhaps into drug or alcohol abuse, or compulsive eating, shopping or exercising. *Oh, it's hopeless*, you think. Corrie ten Boom used to say, "There is no pit so deep but that Jesus' love is deeper still."

If, after reading this chapter, you realize you do have a habit or craving that is out of control, stop and admit your bondage. First to yourself. Then to God.

Now determine to get help—whether it be a Christian counselor, a pastor, or a spiritual friend. Remember, when you call out, the Lord is always there to help and guide you. Never underestimate his power to help you recover. God extends his arms toward you. He waits for you. He is calling and asking you to turn to him.

A former alcoholic who was freed of her bondage told us, "I am on a greater high with the Lord than I ever got on alcohol, and I never have a hangover the next day! I gave him my addiction and he gave me freedom and new life."

PRAYER

Lord, only you can give me the strength I need to overcome this monster that has gripped me in my weakest area. I acknowledge that my addiction is displeasing to you and a snare in my Christian walk. I confess that in the past I have enjoyed it and have been unwilling to lay it down, but I truly desire to overcome it. I don't want to be a slave to this sin. Lord, strengthen me. In Jesus' name, I ask you to enable me today to begin my walk to freedom from this bondage. Thank you, Father. Amen.

ELEVEN

Untwisting Sexuality

The body is not meant for sexual immorality, but for the Lord, and the Lord for the body.... Do you not know that your body is a temple of the Holy Spirit, who is in you, whom you have received from God? You are not your own; you were bought at a price. Therefore honor God with your body.

1 Corinthians 6:13b, 19-20

A brief survey of America's newsstands reveals that ours is a sexually sick society. "Sex sells" is the motto driving the advertising industry, peddling everything from Barbie dolls to shampoo, automobiles to travel tours. Women are exploited and depicted as sex objects. Men are preyed upon and lured to buy products based on sex appeal. And advertising campaigns are only one segment of the bombardment.

I (Ruthanne) saw the following titles displayed on magazine covers at one small airport newsstand. They illustrate just how obsessed with sex our culture really is:

"The Sex Skill Any Woman Can Learn"
"Sex Secrets: How to Deal with It if You Feel Guilty"
"How to Get the Sex Life You Want"
"Masters & Johnson on Flirting and Philandering"
"Staying Young, Smart and Sexy Forever"

This obsession with sex, fed continually by the steady diet of sexually explicit material dispensed by the entertainment industry, produces sick, twisted values. Such distortion implies that seeking sexual gratification is a primary goal of life, an end in itself.

God created sex. But our sexuality is only a part of our whole being. Putting undue focus on *any* part of his creation distorts God's intended plan for our lives. Author Andrew Comiskey gives this clarification of the nature of sexuality:

> It includes a heartfelt yearning for connection with another. At the core it's not a lustful, seductive exercise; it grows from that God-inspired desire within each of us to break out of the walls of the lone self and merge with another human being. Intercourse is only one expression of this merging, albeit the most obvious. Sexuality involves longing and desire. The body longs for human touch; the soul desires a companion to ease its aloneness. Such a yearning is not a concession to our fallenness. According to the Bible, God deemed Adam—prior to the fall—as not suited to being alone (see Gen 2:18). The Creator shaped a complement for Adam to provide for his unique emotional and physical needs, as well as for hers.[1]

Martha is one woman who looked for fulfillment from men, but it always led to a dead-end of disappointment. "I was constantly looking for a man who would love me unconditionally, even after he had learned everything about me," Martha admitted.

If you heard all her story you might conclude that she was in bondage to sex. Actually, Martha was simply searching for the unconditional love she had missed in childhood. But she made the mistake of equating sex with love. She did not realize that truly meaningful intimacy requires the union of her *spirit*, not just her body, with her husband's. When women mistake sex for intimacy, bondage can result.

Once Martha allowed God to heal her in her wounded areas, she was able to contribute to a healthy woman-man relationship. Having a man was no longer her emotional crutch.

HOW DO I LOOK?

From early childhood, girls begin to sense that their physical appearance is related to acceptance and approval by others: "Look pretty, and people like you." From early puberty the message subtly shifts to, "Look sexy, and boys like you." A woman easily assumes that for her to have value as a person she must look a certain way to fulfill others' expectations. The boom in surgical face lifts, "tummy tucks," and breast implants indicates that women have bought into the message.

Author Liz Curtis Higgs points out, "God never says in his Word that he'll love us more if we're thin. Instead, he tells us he loves us unconditionally. God's love really is 'one size fits all!'.... It's encouraging to realize that we don't know the dress size of any of the women in the Bible. On the whole, physical beauty—and especially body dimensions—aren't discussed much in Scripture. He cares about the inside, but we live in a world that is obsessed with the exterior."[2]

PEACE WITH YOUR BODY

Little wonder that many women, Christians included, are confused. On the one hand, the world says, "If it feels good, do it!"—and casts God as an ogre bent on spoiling the fun. On the other hand, public officials decry the frightening increase of sexually transmitted diseases, teen pregnancies, and violent sex crimes. The solution offered in Scripture gets lost in the shuffle, and women ask themselves, *Who am I anyway? Am I only valuable in terms of my sexuality?*

If you struggle with your own sense of self-worth, you are also likely to have ambivalent feelings about your femininity and your sexuality. Author Ingrid Trobisch observes:

> One reason why Christian women especially have such a hard time accepting themselves, including their bodies, is because

the idea still prevails that the spiritual and mental areas of our lives are somehow closer to God, more pleasing to him and more "Christian" than the physical realm. The Bible, which calls the body the "temple of the Holy Spirit" (1 Cor 6:19), says the contrary: the more authentic our faith is, the more we are able to live in peace with our bodies.

... If I do not live in peace with my body, I do not live in peace with my Creator.... It is a well-known fact today that spiritual conflicts can affect a person physically. But we have not yet drawn the opposite conclusion, namely, that physical conflicts can hinder and disturb our spiritual life.[3]

What does it mean to "honor God with my body"? In the context of the verses at the beginning of this chapter, it means to avoid two extremes: Don't be an ascetic, punishing your body in an attempt to sanctify it. However, don't assume that because the spirit is more important than the body you are free to indulge your baser fleshly instincts.

SEARCHING FOR SIGNIFICANCE

As an adult, Tori continually pursued the love that she had missed during her growing-up years. She finally married a dentist who could provide her with prestige and the security of a large home. But both were heavy drinkers, and in a short time both felt trapped in a marriage that had no depth. They soon divorced.

For several years afterward Tori hopped from bar to bar and man to man. "I would wake up in bed with a man I barely knew," she recalls. "I had felt 'special' for a fleeting moment—someone wanted me. But then I'd feel like trash the next morning."

Satan's deception caused Tori to believe that if a man wanted her body, surely he would love her in other ways too. But her downward spiral continued, leading to two pregnancies, two abortions, and the pain of much shame and guilt.

"I believed there was a God, but not that I could know him personally," she says. "I just tried to bury my guilt and go on with life."

Then Russell, a doctor, invited her to be his live-in girlfriend, and her drinking binges again became a way of life. Dark moods would hit Tori whenever she thought of her abortions. One night when she was in one of those moods, Russell ordered her to leave. She agreed, and secretly planned to find a way to kill herself. "I decided I'd end my pain once and for all," she remembers.

Tori threw her things into a suitcase and stormed through the house, headed for the door. But passing through the den she noticed the TV was tuned to a secular program discussing a movie on exorcism. She dropped her suitcase and began to watch the program.

"God used that scene to speak to me. Suddenly I saw it—demons were real, so God must be real too!" she says. "I fell on my knees, tears streaming down my face, as God's awesome presence filled the room. Russell walked in and saw me on my knees. Feeling the Lord's presence, he dropped to his knees beside me. At that moment both of us asked Jesus to come into our lives."

They decided the "right thing to do" as Christians was to get legally married, which they did a month later. But they received no counseling and knew nothing about breaking bondages from past sexual encounters and behavior patterns.

Not surprisingly, Tori's newfound love and joy turned into depression and disillusionment. Within a few months, she was involved in an adulterous relationship. She moved in with yet another man she was sure could make her happy. But of course he couldn't. "For nine months I lived in deceit and sin, once again looking to the wrong source for happiness," she admits.

She saw Russell from time to time and noticed a great change in him; he was so peaceful. "Come on home, Tori. I still love you," he'd say.

Finally his unconditional love drew her back. "I learned he was praying that God would change him—not me. Then I realized I needed to pray for God to change me, not my husband," she said, laughing. "When I first returned I no longer felt any natural love for him, but as I cried out for God to change me, he supernaturally gave me a real love for Russell."

Seeking the Lord together and working at building a healthy marriage, they wanted to have children. But four miscarriages disappointed them. The premature birth and death of their baby daughter, who lived only sixteen days, devastated Tori. By now she had a very successful counseling ministry herself, helping other women who were still trapped in the bondages she had once known.

One of these unmarried women—a beautiful teenage girl she'd helped win to the Lord—called her one night as Tori sat under the Christmas tree lights crying over her lost babies and broken dreams.

"Tori, I've just learned I'm pregnant," the girl said. "But I feel God has told me to give my baby to you and your husband."

What a Christmas gift! What an answer to the many prayers for a baby to hold in her empty arms. Now Tori was crying with happiness. She gave the expectant mother her maternity clothes, and a few months later went with her to the hospital for Samuel's birth. When Tori and Russell took him home their dream at last became a reality. Today eight-year-old Samuel has loving, caring parents who pray over him every day of his life.

"Jesus redeemed my mistakes and restored my dignity as a woman," Tori says. "I now know my heavenly Father's love—the kind of love I was searching for all those years in the arms of men."

SELF-HATRED VS. SELF-ACCEPTANCE

We tell this story because Tori's victory didn't happen overnight, and the same may be true for you. Until she acknowledged and dealt with the root of her problems and became anchored in God's Word through scriptural teaching and guidance, Tori stumbled and made mistakes in her sexual behavior. But finally she was able to take responsibility for her own bad choices—which were rooted in shame and low self-esteem—yet she realized that God loved her and would receive her just as she was. As she submitted to God's ways, the Holy Spirit began the work of changing her from the inside out.

If you see yourself in Tori's story, we suggest you ask yourself these questions: *Have I accepted myself? Or do I strive to perform so others will accept me? Can I appreciate my gifts and acknowledge my limitations? Have I accepted my physical characteristics? Have I accepted my femininity? My sexuality?*

What should be our attitude as Christians toward sexual expression? Psychiatrist and author John White offers this perspective:

> A Christian must bear three things in mind.... First, he must realize that God made his body (including the sexual parts of it) and that he equipped it with a nervous system designed to enable each of us to experience exquisite pleasures....
>
> Second, pleasure is a by-product in life, not a goal.... When we devote our lives to loving obedience to God and to serve one another, we find that the pleasures that eluded us when we made them our goal spring unbidden to surprise us....
>
> Third, sexual pleasure was designed to be enjoyed within marriage. The physical side of sex is only part of a larger whole.... The first purpose of sex is the ending of isolation and loneliness. And loneliness can only end where trust exists—trust that someone has made a commitment to me and I to that person in a sworn covenant until death parts us.[4]

SINGLES AND SEX

The Center for Disease Control in Atlanta tracks more than twenty different dangerous sexually transmitted diseases. And most of those affected are young people—63 percent of STD cases reported are individuals twenty-five years old and younger.[5]

The fear of AIDS and other sexually transmitted diseases is giving rise to a new emphasis on solitary sex. Computer technology is now producing "cybersex." These videos and computer games enable a lone participant to indulge in sexual fantasies and stimuli without becoming vulnerable to an infected partner. It seems that our society is reliving the days of Noah, when "the Lord saw that the wickedness of man was great in the earth, and that every intent of the thoughts of his heart was only evil continually" (Gn 6:5, NKJV).

Sadly, as modern society impacts the church more than the church is impacting society, sexual sin among singles (and infidelity among married people) is becoming an epidemic problem.

Because of the priority placed upon sexual relationships by our society, singles sometimes feel they're only half a person if they don't have a sexual partner. The media besiege us with the message that "good sex" can solve feelings of loneliness, sexual frustration and lack of acceptance. But sex outside marriage is simply not a viable consideration for a Christian, despite the world's message that "everybody's doing it."

The notion that your sexual desires must be fulfilled for you to live is absurd. Without food, water and oxygen you will die. But you will not die if you abstain from sex. Granted, sexual desire may be very strong, accompanied by a longing to bear children and to share affection. But self-control is possible with the help of the Holy Spirit. If it weren't, this prohibition against extramarital sex wouldn't be in Scripture:

> Do you not know that your bodies are members of Christ himself? Shall I then take the members of Christ and unite them with a prostitute? Never! Do you not know that he who unites himself with a prostitute is one with her in body? For it is said, "The two will become one flesh." But he who unites himself with the Lord is one with him in spirit. Flee from sexual

immorality. All other sins a man commits are outside his body, but he who sins sexually sins against his own body.

1 Corinthians 6:15-18

Scripture calls the physical bonding of sexual intercourse "becoming one flesh." But in sexual intercourse (and in other sexual intimacies), the bonding that takes place is both physical and spiritual. Sex creates a "soul tie," an invisible bond which unites the couple in a spiritual sense. For this reason, lovers are sometimes called "soul mates."

Long after the physical act is performed, the bonding of spirits remains. Also, each of the partners is susceptible to the influence of any demonic spirits operating in the life of the other individual. A promiscuous person, or a prostitute, establishes bonds with many different people, resulting in fragmentation of the human spirit and sometimes strong demonic oppression. Such a person needs deliverance and spiritual healing before he or she can establish healthy, godly relationships.

Many Christian singles, driven by frustration, get involved in relationships with non-Christians and often end up marrying them. They ignore the biblical warning, "Do not be yoked together with unbelievers. For what do righteousness and wickedness have in common? Or what fellowship can light have with darkness?" (2 Cor 6:14). Such a marriage could very well set you up for a life of abuse and pain far greater than any pain of loneliness you may feel as a single.

Don't fall for the devil's lie that you would be married if you were attractive enough, talented enough, rich enough, or knew the right people! Minister Michael Cavanaugh, writing to singles, says, "If you wanted to be married today, you could be. I could find somebody for you. If you had no criteria, no real guidelines, or no moral standards to speak of, I could find someone who'd be willing to marry you. Anybody who doesn't have standards can get married."[6]

I (Ruthanne) have heard my wise mother-in-law say many

times, "There's something much worse than not being married—it's being married to the wrong man!"

If you're a single woman who is trusting God for a Christian husband, we encourage you to keep your confidence in God, refuse to compromise your standards, and leave the timing in his hands. God is able to use extravagant means to cause you to meet the mate of his choosing—as he did with Rebekah and Isaac, and with Ruth and Boaz in the Old Testament, for example.

MENTAL ADULTERY

In her book *Feelings Women Rarely Share,* Christian teacher Judy Reamer warns about fantasies—"mental adultery" she calls it. It can be a problem for singles, as well as for married women.

One woman who wrote Judy allowed herself to fantasize as a way to retaliate against a husband who did not meet her emotional needs. Imagining herself dancing, smoking, and drinking, she finally goes to bed with a man she picked up at a bar. Next she began fantasizing about a male acquaintance who expressed interest in her every thought and feeling. He became her ideal—her hero—if only in her dreams. But it's a dangerous game. The "dream" can quickly become a nightmare. Judy says of such fantasy:

> Whether your source of sexual temptation is an old boyfriend, a man on the job, or only someone you have had a dream about, the solution is still the same.... Improper sexual behavior always starts first in the mind.... Therefore, while this solution may sound simplistic—it is still the best answer: STOP THE THOUGHTS! Nip them in the bud.... Do not let your imagination run away with you.
>
> Choose not to review last night's passionate dream. Occupy your mind with organizing your day. Read the Bible, listen to a program on a Christian radio station, or dig out a new recipe for supper. Before long, the sexual thoughts will dissipate....

Remember my little motto, "Affairs start in the head before they get to the bed."[7]

Judy also describes the trap of believing you can liberate a needy man without getting emotionally involved:

Satan loves to deceive believers. When a believer has allowed herself to come under the plan of deception, Satan can use immorality to break down her relationship with God. All too often the deception starts with an innocent involvement with an ungodly man, such as when a married female believer tries to win an unsaved man to the Lord. She may well be on the road marked "this way to hell." Being confident in her own spiritual maturity rather than in God, this woman may travel far down the road before she is rescued.[8]

The apostle Paul urged believers "to offer your bodies as living sacrifices, holy and pleasing to God.... Do not conform any longer to the pattern of this world, but be transformed by the renewing of your mind. Then you will be able to test and approve what God's will is—his good, pleasing and perfect will" (Rom 12:1b, 2).

Meditating on God's Word is the quickest way to resist temptation when it knocks at your mind. Some Scriptures to read include:

Proverbs 6:20-35
Proverbs 9:13-18
Matthew 5:27-28; 19:18
Mark 10:19
1 Corinthians 6:15-20
1 Corinthians 10:1-13
2 Corinthians 12:9
1 Thessalonians 4:1-8
James 2:11
1 John 5:4

CAN GOD HEAL HOMOSEXUALITY?

Maggie's experience answers a resounding "Yes!" to this question, despite secular psychiatrists' claim to the contrary. Growing up as the only girl in a dysfunctional family of five, Maggie felt like the "odd man out" and always wished for a sister. She became a tomboy, hoping her dad would include her in the fishing trips or projects he did with her brothers.

"But he never did," she reports, "and I resented my mother's attempt to feminize me. For me, that meant dresses and uncomfortable shoes, boring housework, and not as much freedom or fun as my younger brothers had. My father was emotionally absent most of the time, and finally my parents divorced back in the sixties. Working hard to support three children on forty dollars a week, my mother suffered unfair treatment as a woman. I resented what I saw happening to her, and my bitterness grew as I went through college and joined the work force myself."

In her job as a newspaper reporter, Maggie saw firsthand many injustices against women in the court system, the school system, in business and banking, and in her own profession. Her solution was to join two other women in forming a chapter of the National Organization for Women, and she became involved with the feminist movement. But within a few months' time this led to her first lesbian relationship. When that alliance failed she stayed in the lifestyle and later became involved in another relationship. Why didn't she learn by her first disappointment? Maggie says:

> I believe it was because of what Dr. Elizabeth Moberley proposes in her study, "Homosexuality: A New Christian Ethic." In seeking a same-sex relationship, homosexuals are attempting to heal some early loss in childhood with the parent of the same sex.
>
> I really cannot blame my parents. Both were children of alcoholics, themselves the early childhood victims of far more harshness than I ever knew. But no one told us we weren't alone—that God was there. His name and prayer had just been excluded from our schools. We were on our own. My generation felt we'd have to reinvent it all—and I tried in all the wrong ways.
>
> I saved women from abusive husbands and saw myself as able to handle anything. Now I know that only God can do

> that. Finally I recognized my real sin—a root of pride and rebellion and a wounded sense of justice—and I was able to humble myself before my God, the only Savior. He healed me from my rebellion and lifestyle in a little church where the goodness of the Lord and his humble people drew me to want to live an honestly righteous life.

Maggie began using her writing skills to report on Christian activities and the work of the Holy Spirit in her community. In doing this she met new friends, but strong temptation entered one of these friendships with a young woman; Maggie fell into another lesbian relationship. She says of that time:

> I chose to walk back into sin, and soon came to a point in my life where I hit bottom: no job, no food, and dependent upon charity to pay my rent. Then one day I heard a TV preacher teach on faith. Feeling almost insane with grief, loss, fear and hunger, I listened for four hours a day for several months. Slowly my faith grew as it was nourished by the Word of God.
>
> Gradually God walked me through the desert of my life to healing. But it was slow this time—not easy like the first experience had been.
>
> I asked God to heal my emotional and psychological wounds with the same power he poured into other people's lives for physical healing. I turned over to him every love affair, every emotional hurt. I had looked for love in many places, but it was wrong to try to heal an emotional hurt with sexual "love." I asked Jesus to lead me to an understanding of Father God such as I'd never had before, and he did that for me.

Maggie believes God heals two ways:

1. By our faith. God grants us the faith to believe he wants to heal us of the things that hurt us, even homosexuality.
2. By his presence. Daily we must stay in the presence of God, who is the only one big enough to heal all the wounds of our past, our present, and our future.

Today Maggie works in a ministry reaching out to hurting women who desire to trust God to help them leave lesbianism behind. God has not led her into a heterosexual relationship and marriage, though that is a future possibility. The important thing is that she is free of the bondage which once held her captive.

It is important to keep in mind that an individual's tendency toward homosexual feelings and the temptation to fulfill them does not constitute sin. It is wrong sexual *behavior* that is sin. No matter what our background or perceived sexual identity, persevering in our relationship with the Lord is our hope for wholeness and spiritual growth. Only the strength he provides enables us to walk in sexual integrity.

USING SEX FOR A "FIX"

Sexual bondage is both a self-image problem and a relationship problem. A woman who depends on a sexual relationship with either gender to maintain self-esteem is not much different from an addict who depends on a substance to keep her going. She is in bondage, using sex for a "fix."

A lot of women seek counseling because they think they have a problem with sex. They soon discover the "sex problem" is a symptom of a deeper problem, which must be identified and dealt with to get free of the bondage. One counselor estimates that 80 percent of the people seeking help for sexual problems actually battle problems related to low self-esteem and poor communication skills.

For many women, masturbation becomes a way of escape from sexual frustration and loneliness. But this practice will not get you out of bondage, and likely will only take you deeper.

Practicing masturbation will no doubt increase your level of shame and guilt for several reasons: it is often accompanied by pornography and illicit fantasies, and can be very addictive. Most significantly, it turns you inward with a focus on gratifying yourself, which defeats the very purpose of sex—an expression of love in a covenant relationship between a husband and wife.

In his discussion regarding masturbation, Dr. White reminds us that God doesn't always deal with all levels of our problems at once. Like untangling a knotted ball of string, certain "knots" have to wait while other tangles are straightened out.[9]

As we concentrate on developing the fruit of the Spirit in our lives—love, joy, peace, patience, kindness, goodness, faithfulness, gentleness, and self-control—we will be less focused on gratifying ourselves (see Galatians 5:22-25). Reaching out to others with God's love and having fellowship with other believers is the antidote for loneliness.

The truth is, no human relationship—whether with a spouse or someone else—can totally fulfill your emotional and spiritual needs. Only a vital relationship with Christ can equip you to establish healthy ties with other significant people in your life. No person can fill the God-shaped void in your spirit that can only be satisfied by your Creator. The psalmist wrote:

> Find rest, O my soul, in God alone;
> my hope comes from him.
> He alone is my rock and my salvation;
> he is my fortress, I will not be shaken. **Psalm 62:5-6**

PRAYER

God, forgive me for the sexual sins I have willingly embraced. Please cleanse me and make me whole, and help me to abstain from evil. My prayer is that you will sanctify me—separate me from profane things, and make me pure and wholly consecrated to you. Lord, may my spirit and soul and body be preserved complete and blameless at the day of your coming. Thank you for setting me free! Amen.[10]

TWELVE

The Bondage of Satan's Counterfeits

> ***The Spirit clearly says that in later times some will abandon the faith and follow deceiving spirits and things taught by demons. Such teachings come through hypocritical liars, whose consciences have been seared as with a hot iron.*** **1 Timothy 4:1-2**

Pick up just about any major newspaper or magazine and you will see that Satan's counterfeits are increasing at an epidemic rate. Feature articles on so-called spiritual topics abound:

- An active New Age community in the California mountains becomes a tourist draw.
- A Texas guest ranch features séances under the guise of "development circles."
- A contingent of Tibetan Buddhist monks takes a prayer journey to major American cities to pray for "the healing of the U.S., the environment, and the human spirit."
- A former Christian minister now offers "spiritual cleansing" sessions at his Indian sweat lodge where he chants incantations to "the Creator."

- "The Earth is our Mother" (a thinly veiled masquerade for goddess worship) becomes a rallying slogan for the ecology movement.
- Advertisements offer a weekend "healing dream" course.
- A survey reveals that 65 percent of Americans between ages eighteen and sixty-four believe that the God of Christians, Muslims, Buddhists, and other groups is the same God but with different names.
- The World Parliament of Religions draws six thousand people from 125 religious groups to a meeting promoting religious harmony, world peace, etc. Christian and Jewish groups participate in pagan ceremonies with Buddhist, Hindu, Sikh, Jain, Taoist, and Muslim representatives.

WEB OF DECEPTION

Why the surge of interest in these spiritual counterfeits? As our society becomes more and more materialistic, more and more violent, false religions and the occult seem to offer desirable solutions. Man is fooled into believing that he can, by "spiritual" means, do anything he sets his mind to. That he can "be like God"—the goal Adam and Eve sought when they ate the forbidden fruit (see Genesis 3:1-19). Man chafes at God's absolutes, refuses to acknowledge his superiority, and will buy into the Serpent's deception because of his pride and rebellion.

One who dabbles in Satan's counterfeits is much like a frog placed in a slowly heating pan of water: unaware of the immediate danger, the frog is scalded to death before he has the sense to jump out of the pot. Helen's experience reveals just how easily one can get caught up—and burned—in deception.

Helen, led by a lust for adventure, rejected her orthodox Jewish upbringing and "innocently" began reading astrology columns. Soon she acquired her own personal astrologist to give detailed guidance for most of her decisions. Then she got involved in a sect of Hinduism and for two years wore nothing but saris.

"I had declared God dead, but was quite open-minded about the occult," she reported. "My friends were dabbling in black magic and witchcraft, and though I was not directly involved, I was tolerant of those who were. I even had a Jungian psychiatrist who practiced divination by using the Chinese *I Ching*. I would acknowledge any god except the true God."

In the course of Helen's spiritual wanderings, her congenital lung disorder worsened and she ended up hospitalized with severe allergies two thousand miles from home. A Christian couple at the hospital shared the love of Jesus with her and opened their home to her.

The wife had an allergy problem similar to Helen's, but during the nine-month stay there Helen saw her hostess, praying and trusting in Scripture, healed of her allergy problems. Helen herself had to return to the hospital, more desperate than ever.

"I needed confirmation that Jesus was real, but I needed it from a non-Christian source," Helen said. "Then my Jewish friend Anne, who was into Hindu philosophies, came to visit and told me of a dream she'd had in which she was crying out for God to heal me. But he told her I would have to ask for myself. Although this was the end of February, she brought me an unusual token—a Christmas card which presented the whole story of Jesus Christ. She said, 'You weren't ready for this two months ago, but now you are.'"

Helen's defenses broke when she realized God used an unbelieving Jew—now a Hindu—to bring her the message of Jesus. It was a turning point. She allowed a Bible study leader to pray for her healing, then she finally acknowledged Jesus as her Messiah. Immediately she was healed of several maladies, and the serious lung problem began improving.

"The person who led me to the Lord took me through the process of forgiving everyone I had any grievance against, and renouncing the occult," she said. "Three weeks after accepting

Jesus, I was baptized in the Holy Spirit and it became clear that more excavating was necessary. The Holy Spirit showed me that my occult past had attracted curses and demons which had to be broken and cast out. One minister prayed with me for three hours until the occult bondage was broken and a new freedom began."

Helen destroyed books and objects which were blatantly occult, and she continued the cleansing of her apartment as the Holy Spirit revealed to her things she needed to get rid of. Now God is using her mightily to minister to others who have been caught in the web of Satan's counterfeits.

THE POLLUTION OF CHRISTIANITY

Occult deception is often subtle and has many faces, some of which are visible even within the church. The infiltration of false teaching into Christian groups is reaching frightening proportions. The incredible reality that so many New Age practices are being taught in the church is surpassed only by the shocking numbers of people who are gullible enough to embrace these heresies. We must give attention to scriptural warnings against being deceived.

A 1993 women's conference promoting goddess worship and "affirming lesbian love-making" drew more than two thousand professing Christians as delegates. It was backed by a coalition of church groups, with primary funding coming from two major denominations.

In the sessions, "leaders rejected the atonement of Jesus Christ, celebrated lesbianism and called for adding books to the Bible. A defining point of the conference was the presentation and use of the name of Sophia... as a feminine name for God," according to the Religious News Service report. A closing worship service featured a ritual using milk and honey, rather than traditional bread and wine, and included the words: "Our Sweet Sophia, we are women in your image."[1]

It seems that "something new" is turning up in religious phenomena almost every week. Yet the roots of these counterfeits are as old as the Garden of Eden. Sadly, we women are amazingly susceptible to the mystique and intrigue of the spirit world. When a prominent wealthy woman introduced Transcendental Meditation in our city, other women clamored around her, eager for participation. They couldn't wait to get on the latest bandwagon. Many of these women called themselves Christians, yet they seemed utterly unable to discern that getting involved in this sort of thing is forbidden by Scripture.

DANGER OF FALSE RELIGIONS

False religions and cults hold a fascination for women yearning for spiritual truth. Julie is an example of a woman who was deceived by a cult because of this yearning. She received little Christian nurturing at home; she attended church sporadically when she and her brother could find a ride with friends. Her desire to know God, along with the insecurities of her childhood, made her easy prey to false doctrine.

Once married, Julie moved into a beautiful new home in a prestigious West Coast neighborhood. "Our neighbors were a wonderful Mormon family who brought us homemade goodies, loaned us their truck, were financially well-established, and didn't smoke or drink," she said. "They were everything I had always wished my parents could have been. When they told me about 'the true restored church of Jesus Christ on earth,' I was interested and began attending church with them."

Julie was drawn to the strong emphasis on family ties, good homemaking skills, and temperance. She and her children attended the church, but her husband wanted no part of it. When their oldest daughter got married in a Mormon Temple, they were barred from attending because they had not taken the necessary oaths.

In studying to prepare for the rites to be admitted to the

Mormon Temple, Julie began to notice things that bothered her. "There was no cross to show they were Christian. There was little emphasis on the Bible. I didn't feel I had gained a closer relationship with Jesus, and their major doctrines seemed to change from time to time. It seemed odd to me that a church that professed to have all the truth would need to change its teachings."

Julie's real eye-opener came when one of her daughters began to date a Christian. His sister confronted Julie one day saying, "Mormons are not Christians!" Then she gave Julie Scriptures on how to test false teachings.

Julie was devastated. She loved Jesus and was living what she thought was a good Christian life. But now she determined to discover truth for herself by reading the Bible and listening to Christian teaching tapes. Then she attended her first Christian worship celebration.

"I had never experienced anything so moving—I could actually feel the Holy Spirit's presence," she reported. "I became so hungry to read the Word! A short time later while visiting a church, when the pastor asked if any wanted to rededicate their lives to Jesus, I practically ran down the aisle to receive prayer. I experienced inexpressible happiness, joy, and peace. At last, my bondage to Mormonism was broken! I have been baptized in water, and now my husband is also following the Lord."

DISTORTIONS OF JESUS

Julie's experience illustrates how easily a sincere person can be deceived and led into bondage if she has no experience of salvation through Christ and little Bible knowledge. For example, the Mormon belief that the Angel Moroni appeared to Joseph Smith (a professing Christian) and told him where to find sacred writings more accurate than the Word of God—such teaching is a red flag for a knowledgeable Christian. We see warnings against these things in Scripture:

Woe to the foolish prophets who follow their own spirit and have seen nothing!... Their visions are false and their divinations a lie. They say, "The Lord declares," when the Lord has not sent them; yet they expect their words to be fulfilled.

Ezekiel 13:3b, 6

The apostle Paul wrote:

I am afraid that just as Eve was deceived by the serpent's cunning, your minds may somehow be led astray from your sincere and pure devotion to Christ.... And no wonder, for Satan himself masquerades as an angel of light. It is not surprising, then, if his servants masquerade as servants of righteousness.

2 Corinthians 11:3, 14-15a

A cult such as the one Julie became involved in is especially dangerous because of its subtlety. Professor and author Michael Green explains:

The cults have many common factors.... They offer us considerable and desirable benefits. They are generally authoritative. They are nearly always led by a personality who is dominant in the cult. They all have a new revelation additional to or replacing Scripture. They all look for total commitment. Many of them have a form of initiation which is little short of indoctrination. Often they profess a secret knowledge revealed only to initiates. And they are very resentful of criticism—quick to intimidate or sue for libel.[2]

It is essential for Christians to use biblical criteria when evaluating any religious group—no matter how morally good it appears to be. Members may quote the Bible, seem to have a reverence for Jesus, or use familiar Christian terms, but you must measure their doctrine against the Word of God.

A key error in cultic groups is denying the necessity of accepting Christ's atoning blood sacrifice for sin as clearly explained in Colossians 1:18-20, Hebrews 2:14-15, and 1 John 1:7. Some may use such terms as "the Christ consciousness" or "oneness with God" or even call Jesus "the Savior" and make you think they are truly Christian. But beware of teachings that imply your good works will earn your salvation, that man goes through stages of reincarnation, or that all people eventually will be saved (universalism).

Avoid any teacher who claims to be the Messiah, or religious groups that claim new written revelation should be added to the Bible. The Scripture gives us these warnings:

> Every word of God is flawless.... Do not add to his words, or he will rebuke you and prove you a liar. **Proverbs 30:5a-6**

> The grass withers and the flowers fall, but the word of our God stands forever. **Isaiah 40:8**

> Jesus answered: "Watch out that no one deceives you. For many will come in my name, claiming, 'I am the Christ,' and will deceive many.... For false Christs and false prophets will appear and perform great signs and miracles to deceive even the elect—if that were possible." **Matthew 24:4-5, 24**

> We have renounced secret and shameful ways; we do not use deception, nor do we distort the word of God. **2 Corinthians 4:2a**

Other Scriptures that will help you:

Psalm 90:1-2
John 1:1, 3, 14
Romans 5:15-17
1 Corinthians 8:6
Galatians 4:4-6
Ephesians 1:19-21
Colossians 2:9
1 Timothy 2:5
1 John 4:3

OPEN DOORS TO DEMONIC INFLUENCE

One of our readers who was once caught in a web of deception wrote to us about it: "I was raised in the church, but grew up playing around with witchcraft and the occult. Last year I was even preparing to become a metaphysical counselor with channeling abilities. Although I was ignorant of the Bible, I would occasionally read it. One day when I read 2 Corinthians 11:14-15 about Satan being an angel of light, it woke me up.

"Channeling leads you to believe that you are merging and communicating with angelic, heavenly spirit guides—your Higher Self, Christ-consciousness and God's Over Soul. In fact, my instructor is convinced that Christ-consciousness is Jesus and the Over Soul is God the Father. After reading those Scriptures I realized I was channeling antichrist consciousness. Since then I have found a church that teaches the Word of God. I realize I opened the door to demonic influence but I know there is victory in Christ Jesus."

This woman's experience illustrates how easily someone can be ensnared by an interest in angels and metaphysical phenomena. We warn you that not all persons who talk about angels and visions are following Christ and basing their beliefs on Scripture. Our reader's letter also raises the question we hear so often, "Can a Christian have a demon?" We've mentioned earlier some of the ways we become vulnerable to the enemy. Let's look at a few examples.

A woman who has been a Christian only two years wrote us concerning her twenty-year-old daughter who is now in a psychiatric hospital because she mutilates her body:

> I puzzled how any form of possession could have happened; then my son informed me that he'd had an experience with the devil in his room when he had been deeply involved in heavy metal music. His sister, who had been a Christian for five years, moved into that same room shortly after my son left home. She

> began to go wild with behavior that was so unlike her. She overdosed on drugs several times, renounced her Christian faith, and refuses to let me visit her in the hospital....

Another wrote about ancestral bondage:

> We are of native American Indian descent. Our ancestors on Mom's side were Indian medicine men who were actively involved in their way of worship. Demon spirits have been present throughout my thirty-seven years. I have been taught to memorize a lot of curses. My mom is possessed by many demons, and she hears voices in her head. She recently tried to kill me with a knife. I give myself to the Lord—my mind, heart, body and soul in Jesus' name. I need help with my self-esteem, and forgiving myself for unforgivable acts in anger and resentment.

These are only a few of the scores of people we've heard from who need help to get free from satanic bondage. In the process of helping them it is important for us to distinguish the difference between renouncing the practices of heavy metal rock groups, channelers, Indian medicine men, and so forth, and rejecting the people who are caught in these deceptions and need deliverance.

We should reach out in love to Native American people, but not participate in or condone their pagan rites and ceremonies. We should not insist that they renounce their entire culture—only those elements of the culture which are incompatible with Scripture. Too many in our society have done the opposite—embraced elements of a culture's false religion, while rejecting the people on an individual basis. If we thoroughly explored our own roots, probably we would find that demonic-related customs and traditions are in our background too.

Charles H. Kraft, anthropology professor at Fuller Theological Seminary, addresses this important issue concerning converts to Christianity who bring with them demonic influences from their backgrounds:

A certain number of Christian converts come out of occult backgrounds. Marvelous conversion experiences prompt them to seek church membership. Unfortunately, we have lost the early church tradition of cleansing new converts of demonic infestation before they join, so they usually come into membership carrying some or all of the demons they once served. Though the demons are weakened because they have lost the spiritual center of the person, they hang on in mind, body, emotions, and will. From those positions they can continue to disrupt both the life of the convert and those to whom the convert relates.... Demons in Christians are usually left over from their non-Christian past. I have, however, dealt with many demons that have been allowed in by Christians during lapses in their Christian lives.

... I conclude, therefore, that demons cannot live in that innermost part of Christians, their spirit, since it is joined to and filled with the Holy Spirit (Rom 8:16). That part of Christians becomes alive with the life of Christ and is inviolable by representatives of the Enemy. Demons can, however, live in a Christian's mind, emotions, body, and will.[3]

PROTECT YOUR HOME

Any artifacts—music albums, videos, computer games, books, posters, writings, paintings, ceremonial articles or clothing, statues, jewelry—that give glory to violence, the occult, or any of Satan's counterfeit guises are dangerous for Christians to have in their homes (see Deuteronomy 7:25-26).

Scripture gives this account of what happened when Paul preached in Ephesus:

Many also of those who had believed kept coming, confessing and disclosing their practices. And many of those who practiced magic brought their books together and *began* burning them in

t of all; and they counted up the price of them and
it fifty thousand pieces of silver. **Acts 19:18-19, NASB**

To safeguard your home you should:

1. Commit your home to the Lord. Anoint the doors and doorposts of your house with oil as an outward symbol that you are dedicating it to God and petitioning him for the safety of those who dwell there.
2. Pray over your family members at night—ask for health and safety—even if you do it after they are asleep.
3. Remove from your house and destroy any pornography, New Age or occult toys, games, music, videos, disks, books, posters, or any artifacts associated with false religions, cults, or occult practices.
4. Ask the Holy Spirit to reveal to you any specific spirits to be cast out (see Mark 9:25). Address any and all spirits associated with any objectionable things you once had in your house. Command them to depart in the name and authority of Jesus Christ, and remind them that they have no right to remain.

Women married to unbelievers often aren't free to destroy things belonging to their husbands or their in-laws, though they know the items are an abomination to the Lord. But they can bind the spirits associated with those objects and in the name and power of Jesus Christ nullify their evil power.

When it comes to your children, you can keep them from listening to rock music, watching occult shows on TV—even cartoons. They are under your authority until the legal age of adulthood in your state, and subject to you while they live in your home. This must be taken seriously if you want your home cleansed.

Once while I (Quin) was visiting in a friend's home, my friend had a revelation in the night that her son was hiding pornography in the house. While I prayed she took a flashlight and searched until she found his stack of magazines, then she destroyed them. Since he was still living under her roof she believed she had the authority and responsibility before God to cleanse the house of this evil.

OCCULT DIVINATION

What is the difference between the occult and the cults? The word occult means "hidden, secret, not able to be seen or detected." The term the occult refers to "matters involving the action or influence of supernatural agencies or some secret knowledge of them."[4] When we Christians speak of a cult we mean an exclusive religious group whose beliefs and practices are deviant from the mainstream of Christianity. (Thus an "occult cult" is possible.)

"Astrology [seeking to foresee or foretell the supposed influence of stars and planets on human affairs] is the most popular form of occult divination in America today," states an article in *The Watchman Expositor*. The item includes research which claims that there are "over 10,000 professional astrologers in the U.S. with a clientele of over 20 million people," and that "32 million Americans believe in astrology."[5]

The roots of astrology go back to the worship of the sun, moon, stars, and planets by the ancient Chaldeans of Babylonia. Isaiah 47:13 refers to astrologers and stargazers when the prophet taunts the Babylonians to go to these powerless predictors for their salvation. (Don't confuse astronomy, the scientific study of the solar system and the movement of the stars and planets, with astrology.)

A horoscope (from Greek roots meaning "watcher of the hour") is a chart from which astrological predictions are made for an individual based on time of birth.[6] Consulting an astrologer or a printed horoscope for guidance is forbidden by Scripture. One commentary states:

Going to the stars for guidance was the same as idolatry to biblical writers. Samuel equated the two in his denunciation of Saul (1 Sm 15:23).

... The Bible's contempt for astrology is most clearly seen in its prohibition of any technique to aid in predicting the future. Astrology assumes that God does not control history. It assumes that history is governed by the affairs of the pagan gods as revealed in the movement of the planets. The believer knows that a sovereign God rules this world. He also knows that resorting to astrology is a denial of the life of faith by which one trusts God and not his lucky stars for the future.[7]

RECOGNIZE AND REPENT

The Bible says, "Let no one be found among you who sacrifices his son or daughter in the fire, who practices divination or sorcery, interprets omens, engages in witchcraft, or casts spells, or who is a medium or spiritist or who consults the dead. Anyone who does these things is detestable to the Lord" (Dt 18:10-12a).

One Bible teacher's suggestion concerning any occult participation either by us or our forefathers is that we ***recognize, repent, renounce*** and ***resist*** it.

To recognize any occult involvement, ask yourself whether you or members of your family have ever:

- had your fortune told—by crystal ball, cards, *I Ching,* tea leaves, tarot cards, palm reading, Ouija board, planchette, signs of zodiac—even "in fun."
- read horoscopes, consulted an astrologist, or participated in any form of astrology.
- participated in transcendental meditation or any kind of passive meditation.
- been involved in hypnosis.

- been involved in séances, consulting mediums, or attending spiritualist meetings.
- studied or participated in New Age, channeling, or Edgar Cayce, Jean Dixon, Shirley MacLaine philosophies.
- gone to an Indian sweat lodge or participated in "cleansing ceremonies" or other such rituals.
- communicated with demons impersonating people (trying to contact the dead).
- been involved in any cult religion such as Mormon, Unity, Religious Science, Science of Mind, Christian Science.
- been a part of any secret society (such as Masons, Eastern Star, Rainbow Girls) or taken oaths contrary to the Word of God.
- been involved in any martial arts in which you bowed or paid homage to another god or being as part of the ceremony.
- participated in any form of yoga.
- taken any mind-altering drugs such as LSD or angel dust.
- participated in "automatic writing."
- participated in "water-witching" or used clairvoyance in any way to find water, lost objects, and so forth.
- participated in levitation or astral projection.
- owned any occult or psychic objects, "sacred writings" or artifacts of other gods (i.e. images or drawings of Buddha, Hindu deities, Tiki dolls, voodoo dolls, fetishes...).
- watched TV programs, videos, or movies promoting the occult.
- sought cures through such means as psychic healing, acupuncture, iridology, reflexology, or other forms of holistic folk medicine.
- played with games of an occult nature such as *Dungeons and Dragons, E.S.P., Telepathy, and Kabala.*

To receive cleansing from these defilements you need to do the following, preferably when you can have a prayer partner with you: (See the prayers at the end of the chapter.)

1. Confess your faith in Jesus Christ as the Son of God and declare aloud, "The shed blood of Jesus sets me free from Satan's power!"
2. Confess your involvement with the occult, naming the practices in which you participated.
3. Speaking aloud, renounce Satan and all demonic forces and command them to depart from you.
4. Ask forgiveness for any anger or root of bitterness so the enemy will have no foothold in your life (see following chapter).
5. Accept God's forgiveness and seek his help in walking free without turning again to demonic influences.

UNHOLY SHRINES

A mother brought her unusually fearful young daughter to a church counseling team that my friend Betty leads, asking for prayer. As soon as they began to pray Betty felt the problem was connected with the occult. "Have you ever taken your daughter into any unholy places which could have caused occult bondage?" she asked.

"Yes, while my husband was stationed in Japan we toured Buddhist shrines; she was with us," the mother confessed.

"Are you willing to ask the Lord to forgive you for that?"

"Yes, of course!" the woman replied. "It was innocent. We're Christians—we didn't know we were doing anything wrong."

After the mother's prayer of confession and repentance, Betty prayed to release the child from demonic bondage. They left that prayer session with a happy little girl who was no longer plagued with tormenting fear.

"Is this for real?" you may ask. Yes, in this instance, the child was attacked when the parents, nominal Christians, unknowingly exposed their daughter (and themselves) to demonic influence.

What if you are required by your job or for research purposes to visit places you know are unholy? It is important to pray for the Lord's protection in advance, then renounce and break off all demonic forces when you leave the place.

PRAYERS TO HELP YOU

In addition to praying these prayers to confess and renounce occult involvement, to cleanse your house, to break unholy ties, etc., you should also declare God's Word over the lives of your family and yourself, using appropriate Scriptures. (See our book *The Spiritual Warrior's Prayer Guide*.) Don't just renounce the negative; replace it with the positive. Also, it is important to have seasons of praise and worship as you exalt Jesus and his lordship in your life. It's also advisable to play tapes or CDs of praise music and recitations of Scripture in your home, because it is a sanctuary of the Lord's presence.

> *Father, I confess my occult involvement as sin—those actions I remember* (name them out loud) *and those I do not remember—and I ask for your forgiveness. I repent of these acts and renounce them as an abomination to you. I consider all things of Satan to be wrong and I close the door in my life on all occult practices. By the authority of Jesus Christ—in his name and by the power of his blood—I command all evil spirits to cease their harassment and to leave* NOW.
>
> *Lord, I ask you to break any occult bondage or oppression in our family history, and to free me and my family and future generations from occult influences through the blood of the Lord Jesus Christ. I give you praise, mighty God, and thank you for the victory. Amen.*

...tan, I have confessed my past involvement in your evil works, and I command you and your emissaries to leave me and my property in the name of Jesus Christ. As an act of my will, I close the door to you forever. I renounce you and cleanse my home of all objects related to your dark kingdom. Because the blood of Jesus has broken the curse and stripped you of your weapons, I am now free from your hold on my life.

I declare the lordship of Jesus Christ rules and reigns in my life, my mind, my emotions, and my home, and his blood covers me and my family; my household is under the protection of the Almighty God.

Lord, forgive me for any wrong emotional ties I have had with (relatives, secret societies, close friends, or cults), *even those I can't presently recall. I renounce those I can remember* (name them). *I repent for these unhealthy alliances, and in receiving the Lord's forgiveness I declare I am cleansed from them by the shed blood of the Lord Jesus Christ. Because his blood has broken the curse and stripped the enemy of his power, I am now free from any hold these ties have had on my life. Lord, I choose to walk in obedience to your Word. I give you praise in Jesus' name. Amen.*

The following prayer to break curses was sent to us by one of our readers and intercessors:

Father, I confess the sins committed by me and my ancestors that have introduced curses into my family line. I rebuke, break, and loose myself and my family line of my own sins and the iniquities of my ancestors or any other person that may have resulted in a curse. I am redeemed by the blood of the Lamb.

I break the power of every spoken curse that has come from my own mouth. I take back the ground I have yielded to the devil and claim blessings instead. I break the power of every evil word spoken knowingly or unknowingly against me and cancel the power of that curse in the name of the Lord Jesus.

I break every oath, chant, incanation, hex, pact, bondage, spell, voodoo, satanic art or practice, negative agreement or confession cast over me and my family regarding the (name the curse) *in the name of the Lord Jesus Christ. Your power is shattered and returned to the source. Every avenue is now closed to you in the name and by the blood of the Lord Jesus Christ.*

THIRTEEN

What Happens When You Don't Forgive

Then the master called the servant in. "You wicked servant," he said, "I canceled all that debt of yours because you begged me to. Shouldn't you have had mercy on your fellow servant just as I had on you?"

Matthew 18:32-33

Forgiveness through Christ is the cornerstore of our reconciliation and relationship with God. Knowing this, Satan attacks our capacity to give and receive forgiveness. He provokes us to indulge our grievances and hold on to our bitterness by telling us over and over, "The person who did this to you doesn't deserve to be forgiven!"

Only Christ's sacrifice has the power to free us from sin and its bondage. Yet Jesus fixed a condition for that freedom in his parable of the unmerciful servant. In this story the king represents God and the servants represent us, his children.[1]

The first servant, without money or assets, owed the king a huge sum of money—more than he could possibly earn in a lifetime. The king, following the common practice of the day, ordered the man and his family sold into slavery to settle the debt.

When the servant cried out for mercy the king chose to forgive the entire debt, and released the man.

But on the way home, this forgiven man met a fellow servant who owed him a small amount of money—a mere fraction of the sum just taken off his own record. Ignoring his king's example of mercy, he grabbed his fellow servant by the throat and demanded immediate payment. He refused the man's plea for mercy and had him thrown into prison until he could pay.

The king heard of the incident, angrily reprimanded the wicked servant, then ordered him put in jail until he could pay the full amount of what he had owed. One translation says the king "delivered him to the tormenters..." (v. 34, KJV).

It's no accident that this scenario portrays the unforgiving servant as being in prison. It's as true today as it was on the day Jesus taught the parable. Unwillingness to forgive will sentence you to bondage and torment, and the person you refuse to forgive remains bound also.

A PRISON WITHOUT BARS

What fruit does unforgiveness bear? It keeps us in bondage to hurts and memories of the past. It stifles joy and poisons relationships. It even makes us susceptible to physical illnesses.

Once, after I (Ruthanne) had finished teaching a home Bible study in Singapore, a small, forlorn woman I'll call Ellen came up to me. "Please pray for me," she said. "I have pain in my chest and it's difficult to breathe." Before beginning to pray as she had requested, I felt impressed to ask God how he wanted me to pray (I've learned this is a useful thing to do in most cases). The Holy Spirit whispered to me that she had a problem with unforgiveness.

"Ellen, before I pray I need to ask you a question," I said. "Is there someone in your life who has wronged you in some way? Someone toward whom you feel bitter and angry?"

Her lips tightened as she dropped her head. "Yes," she said

softly, "my sister-in-law. She has spoken bitter words against me."

I began sharing with her several Scriptures on the importance of forgiving anyone who had hurt her, explaining that this was the key to her freedom. As I talked she stared at the floor, unable to look me in the eye.

"But I can't forgive her," she said, shaking her head. "She has spoken against me like this for years. She is cruel and mean to me."

Ellen, a single woman, said she was forced by circumstances to live with her brother and his wife. She wept as she shared how the sister-in-law verbally abused her, treating her like a servant, while her brother did nothing to defend her.

"Ellen, I believe your chest pain and breathing problems are caused by the emotional pain you feel," I said. "Jesus loves you, and it is not his will for you to remain in this bondage. Your sister-in-law's behavior is wrong, but she treats you this way because she is also in bondage. The key to your being healed is for you to forgive her. And Jesus can help you to do that."

Silently praying for wisdom, I reviewed with her the parable of the unmerciful servant, emphasizing that his refusal to forgive a fellow servant caused both of them to remain in a tormenting prison. "If you don't forgive, you will continue to suffer," I explained. "But if you tell the Lord you are willing to forgive, and ask the Holy Spirit to help you, he will enable you to begin that process. He only wants your willingness to obey him one step at a time."

Nothing I said seemed to penetrate the wall that Ellen's pain had built around her heart. She kept shaking her head back and forth, weeping and saying, "I can't, I can't."

Finally I asked the Lord to continue speaking to her through the Word and to give her his strength to obey it. I prayed for the Holy Spirit to comfort her in her pain. But I could not pray for her physical healing. With an aching heart I watched her walk out of the meeting as sick as when she had come in. She truly was a woman in a prison without bars, but she was there by choice.

THE FRUIT OF UNFORGIVENESS

In Paul's letters he cautioned believers against harboring unforgiveness toward others, because it opens a door to the enemy. He wrote:

> In your anger do not sin: Do not let the sun go down while you are still angry, and do not give the devil a foothold.... Get rid of all bitterness, rage and anger, brawling and slander, along with every form of malice. Be kind and compassionate to one another, forgiving each other, just as in Christ God forgave you.
>
> Be imitators of God, therefore, as dearly loved children and live a life of love, just as Christ loved us and gave himself up for us as a fragrant offering and sacrifice to God.
>
> **Ephesians 4:26-27, 31-32; 5:1-2**

The negative behavior and attitudes mentioned in verse 31 all have to do with human relationships. Paul was writing to Christians here, but it is clear by his language that they needed to deal with the grievances and hard feelings they had toward one another. He reminds them that forgiving each other, following Christ's example, is the solution to their conflicts as well as their protection against the devil's strategy. And it's our protection, too.

Continual, unresolved conflict with a difficult person can seriously traumatize your life. It may cause or contribute to chronic physical problems such as asthma, ulcers, arthritis, migraines, and muscle spasms. Or it may show up in emotional problems such as panic attacks, learning disabilities, eating disorders, etc.

Paula struggled for nineteen years with panic attacks. Whenever she would get in crowds she would break out in a cold sweat and her heart raced so fast she felt she would explode. Doctors call this condition agoraphopia—based on the Greek word agora, meaning marketplace. The person who suffers with it is fearful of being in places or situations from which escape might be difficult or embarrassing, or where he or she has no control over the surrounding circumstances.

In restaurants, Paula would insist that her husband sit with her near an exit door and gulp down his food as fast as she did, so they could get out as quickly as possible. She decided to go to church, thinking that might help. She went alone, sat on the back pew—and left early when a sense of panic would overwhelm her. She never lasted through an entire service. If she ever ventured into a grocery store she'd only go through the express line, and even then sometimes would throw down her items and run from the store. She couldn't travel on an airplane, ride an elevator, or go to see her two daughters participate in school programs.

Four pills a day for her nerves seemed to have minimal effect. Her husband Ben was her emotional crutch; he would call from work several times a day to check on her. "I'll always be here for you, Paula," he would say. "I'll never leave you." But one day Ben told her he needed his freedom, and walked out on her. For five years he kept saying, "I'm coming back—just give me a little more time."

As Paula's world crumbled around her, she met a Christian who befriended her and led her to the Lord. "I could call Beverly any time—day or night—when a panic attack would hit," Paula reported. "She offered love and acceptance and would always pray with me, but she was never pushy. After I received Jesus into my heart she began teaching me about forgiveness, and that started me on the road to healing.

"For years I had harbored bitterness and hatred toward my Jewish mother-in-law, Miriam. I had married her only child, and I was not a Jew. She didn't like me and I didn't like her. When we moved to New York, Ben moved his parents too. Every weekend we had them over. She told me how to raise my girls, how to cook, how to keep house. She was always on my case—it seemed I had no control over my own life. When her belligerent attitude got the best of me I started having panic attacks, but it never occurred to me that there was a cause-and-effect relationship.

"It was a long time before a counselor told me it was agoraphobia. But he could only give me the name, not the cause or a cure, and prescribe tranquilizers."

BREAKING THE BONDAGE

When Paula made the difficult decision to forgive her mother-in-law, the Lord gave her a supernatural love for this woman who was otherwise quite unlovable. And she began reaching out to her, showing concern for her welfare.

The panic attacks did not disappear immediately, but her prayer partner, Beverly, gave Paula a "prescription" to follow for the panic attacks. Every day before leaving the house she would quote, "I can do all things through Christ who strengthens me" (Phil 4:13, NKJV), then she would pray, "Come, Holy Spirit... go with me." She found a solid, supportive church and began to grow in the Lord. The panic attacks began diminishing, and Paula hoped all these positive changes in her would influence her husband to return.

"During prayer I kept hearing the word 'restoration,' and thought this meant God would restore our marriage," Paula shared. "I cried every weekend and finally prayed, 'Lord, if you're not going to bring Ben back, please take this terrible ache out of my heart.' The Lord sovereignly did that. I still wanted him back, but the ache was gone."

After five years of separation, Ben told Paula that he was in love with a woman twenty years younger, and asked for a divorce so he could marry her. Then Paula learned that Miriam had known about her son's affair all along, and had encouraged the relationship. It was a disappointing blow, but this time she had her faith in the Lord to sustain her.

"I realized I had to forgive Ben for giving me false hope all those years, and I also had to forgive the other woman," she said. "Ben moved his mother to a retirement center and she gave almost all her possessions to his new wife, so I had more mother-in-law forgiving to do. It was not easy, but I knew this was the way Jesus would do it. I wanted to be right before the Lord, and I didn't want to fall back into the bondage I had been in before.

"I asked Ben to forgive me for my part in the bad marriage, and told him I forgave him for leaving me. It took him off-guard, but he received it. I continued reaching out to Miriam, and I forgave her for encouraging Ben's affair."

HEALING AND RECONCILIATION

Paula was astonished one day when Miriam called from where she now lived several hours away and said, "Can I come to visit you for a few days? I want to see your new apartment." Paula urged her to come, realizing this would truly be a test of her emotional healing.

"It was amazing how all the anger and bitterness I had felt for years toward my Jewish mother-in-law was now replaced by a genuine love for her," she said. "'Mother Mim' stayed for a week and we had a wonderful time together. She cried and apologized for giving most of her things to Ben's new wife, but she did give me a diamond dinner ring that had been one of her dearest treasures. She went with me to church and to Bible study and I gave her a Bible. My pastor prayed for her, and the people showed her such love she said, 'If I lived here, this would be my church.' She didn't yet know Jesus, but she responded to our love."

After Miriam returned to the retirement center, Paula and a team from the church began driving down to visit her and they organized Bible studies at the center. A short time later, at age eighty-six, Miriam received Jesus as her Messiah and joyfully served the Lord for the next two years before she died.

"Ben and his new wife haven't yet come to the Lord, but they occasionally call me for prayer," Paula continued. "Ben told me I could call on him for financial help if I had problems making it on my limited Social Security income. I asked for help a few times, and it was comforting to know it was available. But then I felt the Lord wanted me to trust him completely to meet my needs—otherwise my relationship with Ben and Elise would be tainted.

"I began reading about provision in the Bible, and began to claim the promise in Psalm 128:1-2: 'Blessed is every one who fears the Lord, who walks in his ways. When you eat the labor of your hands, you shall be happy, and it shall be well with you' (NKJV). I had never done anything artistic with my hands—never felt I had any creative talent. But the Lord opened the door for me to start my own handcraft business decorating T-shirts and sweatshirts, and I have been inundated with orders. A lawyer friend is helping me with the legal paperwork, and I absolutely love what I am doing.

"Ben can scarcely believe that I am successfully living on my own and starting my own business—all without any help from him. It's a wonderful testimony of my complete healing—a woman who a few years ago could barely manage a trip to the grocery store without help."

Paula told us she asked both her daughters to forgive her for not having been the mother they needed, and she also convinced Ben to apologize to the older daughter because he had been so verbally abusive toward her. "I am trusting God to heal all the hurts my girls have suffered, and to reveal his love to them. Then my own relationship with them can be restored."

THE POWER OF ONE PERSON'S DECISION

Paula's story is a striking example of the destructive toll unforgiveness exacts from people's lives. She suffered emotionally and physically, lost her marriage, and was alienated from her daughters and mother-in-law before someone shared God's love with her and healing began. She attributes these losses to the root of bitterness she harbored against her mother-in-law.

But Paula's experience also illustrates that one person's decision to forgive has power to open prison doors for those in hopeless bondage. Because she forgave, her mother-in-law is in heaven today. She herself is healed and now able to touch other women's lives with healing. She refuses to wallow in regret; instead she rejoices in her freedom.

Jesus declared, "The thief comes only to steal and kill and destroy; I have come that they may have life, and have it to the full" (Jn 10:10). Paula can testify that the thief—Satan—almost succeeded in destroying her. But since she received Jesus' life and began to obey his Word, she has begun to live a full and meaningful life.

STEPS IN FORGIVING

Perhaps the most important thing to understand about forgiving is this: it is almost always a process, more than an isolated occurrence. A counselor friend tells her clients they first need to "own up to their feelings," and then forgive so that God can set them completely free.

"We might make a blanket statement like, 'I forgive my father,' but we need to forgive specifically," she says. Her suggestion is that in prayer you say something more explicit, such as: "God, I forgive Dad for not being there when I needed him; for touching me improperly; for beating me, for not showing love; for being mean to my mom; for dying and abandoning me..." or whatever the situation.

In some cases it's helpful to make a list of everything you didn't get or didn't get enough of from your mother, father, husband, or whoever wounded you. Or you may need to list all the reasons you are still angry at that person. Then for each circumstance, go to God in prayer and forgive specifically the things you have listed.

If possible, it is beneficial to talk these things over with a counselor or a prayer partner, and to have them pray with you. Sharing with a person you can trust helps you to give vent to your feelings, an important step in the process. It also makes you accountable to someone who can help you see the situation objectively.

As you follow these suggested steps you are releasing from your own judgment the person who has offended you, and leaving it up to God to judge him or her. Thus both of you can be set free from the bondage of unforgiveness.

1. Acknowledge the wounding you have suffered because of this person's actions toward you; tell the Lord exactly how you feel. Don't be afraid to admit that you are angry about the loss he or she has caused in your life.
2. Choose to forgive the person who has hurt you. This is an act of your will—a decision, not an emotion. Follow Jesus' example of refusing to retaliate (see 1 Peter 2:23).
3. Pray, "Lord, help me to look at this person from your point of view, and to love him or her with your love" (see Romans 5:5). Then seek his guidance as to if and when you should contact the person—by phone or letter, or in person—to say, "I forgive you." If the person doesn't know he has wounded you, ask God whether it is appropriate for you to offer him or her forgiveness.

   Sometimes it is better that you just tell God you forgive that other person. This kind of forgiveness is often necessary when the person who hurt us is dead.

   Keep in mind that forgiving your offender does not mean you must continue to be vulnerable to abuse. Unless the person shows remorse, reconciliation will not likely be possible.
4. Thank God for forgiving you. Your sin against him was much greater than this person's offense against you (see Romans 4:7-8).
5. Thank God for the blessings you've received from this person. Ask him to show you what they are if necessary (see Philippians 4:8). For example: Perhaps your husband betrayed you

or abused you. Yet you can thank God for the children you have because of him.

6. Recognize that this person had a great need in his life when he hurt you; wounded people wound others. Use Jesus' prayer in Luke 23:34 as a model.
7. Pray for the person; bless, don't curse. It's difficult to retain your bitter feelings when you're blessing him and praying for him to be set free (see Luke 6:28, 35).
8. Remember that your forgiving that person is a condition for your own continued forgiveness and spiritual growth (see Matthew 6:14-15).
9. Ask God to forgive you for the anger and resentment you've had toward him because you feel he allowed the offense to happen. It was not God's will for you to suffer, but he could not overrule the offender's right to exercise his free will in doing what he did.
10. Then, best of all, tell the Lord, "I receive your forgiveness! Thank you for cleansing me from my sins. Thank you that I am free of that bondage."
11. Determine that you will no longer dwell on the hurts of the past. When those thoughts and feelings come, declare to the enemy, "That is forgiven and under the blood of Jesus! I close the door on those old hurts once and for all." And finally, don't keep talking about it. As one pastor said, "Stop nursing and rehearsing your hurts."

Bible commentator Herbert Lockyer writes:

If ours has been a mere intellectual acceptance of the doctrine of the forgiveness of sin, but conduct and character remain unchanged and our heart is hard toward others, the Lord will deliver us to the tormentors. He will leave us to the upbraidings of our conscience, or assaults of Satan, until we are brought to act in conformity with His will and example. We are to behave toward others as God behaves toward us. If we claim to be His, then we must have His disposition to forgive, even our enemies. Thus merciful, we can expect to obtain mercy (Matthew 5:7).[2]

PRAYER TO RELEASE FORGIVENESS

If you recognize your own need to forgive someone who has offended you, use this prayer as a guideline:

Father, you see my situation and the pain I have suffered because of (name's) *words and actions against me. I confess to you that I have harbored unforgiveness in my heart toward him (her). I acknowledge this as sin and ask for your forgiveness and cleansing.*

I choose to forgive (name) *for* (name the offenses)*, and I release him (her) from my judgment. Lord, help me to see* (name) *and his (her) needs from your point of view. I ask you to judge him (her) according to your mercy, and to grant him (her) healing and release from bondage.*

Thank you, Father, that even though it's sometimes hard for me to realize, blessings have come to my life because of (name). *One is that I am learning the power of forgiveness. I pray you will release your blessings into his (her) life, and that he (she) will acknowledge them as coming from you. Thank you for forgiving me. Lord, help me to love with your love, and to continue to walk in forgiveness. I ask this in Jesus' name. Amen.*

FOURTEEN

Forgiving Sets You Free

For if you forgive men when they sin against you, your heavenly Father will also forgive you.

Matthew 6:14

So if the Son sets you free, you will be free indeed.

John 8:36

Freedom. Everybody longs for it, but true freedom is available only through Christ. The question is, are we willing to fulfill God's primary condition: forgiving those who have offended us?

"Are you kidding?" may be your response. "You don't know what they did to me. I could never forgive them!"

Exactly what does it mean to forgive? The word has several shades of meaning:

1. to absolve from payment of (to cancel a debt)
2. to excuse from a fault or an offense
3. to renounce anger or resentment against
4. to give up the wish to punish or to get even
5. to bestow a favor unconditionally
6. to release, set at liberty, unchain.

Reading a dictionary definition of the meaning of to forgive is one thing; actually doing it on a daily basis is quite another. Our enemy knows that when we choose to forgive we are released from bondage, and his goal is to keep us in captivity. Recognizing the devil's strategy to keep you bound is the first step to your freedom.

FINDING WHOLENESS THROUGH FORGIVENESS

Marie is a young married woman whose quest for freedom and wholeness led her on a path to forgiveness.

"God, more than anything else, I want to be whole. I want to be consistent in you—not always feeling up and down, depending on circumstances," Marie prayed as she grappled with the conflict between her innermost feelings of brokenness and the happy Christian image she projected outwardly.

> My concept of God was colored by my relationship with my dad, and I always felt he was a little bit mad at me. His goal in life had been to become a priest, but in high school he met my mother and married her instead. Early in the marriage she was unfaithful to him, and during the time she was pregnant with me she had one affair after another. Shortly after my birth Dad divorced her, then sent me to live with his mother. He was bitter over giving up his dream of becoming a priest, only to suffer the shame of his wife's unfaithfulness and to be left with the responsibility of a little baby.
>
> About two years later he married his secretary, Darlene, and brought me into their home. Darlene had suffered much abuse in her life—probably sexual abuse too. Unable to bear children of her own, she resented me intensely. I looked just like my mother, and to her I represented my father's first love. She had no idea how to rear a child—nor how to deal with the strong emotions I evoked in her. Dad was too busy climbing the success ladder in banking even to notice his forlorn little girl.

Over the next fifteen years Marie's life was filled with abuse and cruelty. Darlene berated her, saying she was ugly and stupid. She would grab and beat Marie for no apparent reason—sometimes hitting her face until her mouth bled—then make her lie to explain the bruises and scars. Marie recalled:

> In kindergarten I began stealing things from other children. I'd take them home and say, "Look, Mommy—I got this for being good."
>
> But the item often had another child's name on it. My ploy to win approval backfired, causing even more abuse. By age thirteen I was so empty of any kind of affection, I was vulnerable to the first boy who showed any interest in me.
>
> Once I lost my virginity, I bounced from one relationship to another, giving myself to anyone who offered what I thought was love. Though the emptiness and pain of rejection made me wish I could die, fear kept me from killing myself. I'd been taught that if you commit suicide you go straight to hell, and I really wanted to be with Jesus in heaven and have him love me. But I never thought I was good enough for that.

Have you ever felt as if you were barely existing in a sort of "twilight zone" like Marie's—afraid to die, but finding life unbearable? Seeking ways to stop her pain, Marie studied ballet and art and also got involved in the hippie movement.

At age fifteen she began dating a college student when he came home on weekends. In order to use the family car for their dates, his Christian parents required him to attend church on Sunday. Attending her boyfriend's church on their dates, Marie heard the message of salvation in a way she'd not understood before.

"I can't tell you what it meant to me when I found out that Jesus loved me just as I was, and that I could actually go to heaven to be with him," she said. "I stood up in that church and accepted Jesus into my heart. My boyfriend yanked on my arm and said, 'You're crazy—don't do that!' I had no opportunity to be discipled or nurtured, so I quickly fell back into sinful behavior. But something happened in my heart that day that I never forgot."

Marie went off to college still following the hippie lifestyle of her peers, yet in her confusion she often prayed, "Jesus, I hope you love me...." Then her father told her he was divorcing Darlene and marrying another woman. Marie had mixed feelings—happy he was getting rid of the mother who had abused her; guilty about feeling that way. And a sense of guilt caused her to believe she was now responsible to look after Darlene, who by now had become an alcoholic and a drug addict.

Marie remembers that time as a turning point in her life:

> I wanted desperately for my dad to look at me and say, "I love you," or to show some interest in my welfare. But he, too, had become an alcoholic, and in the pursuit of his own happiness he couldn't see my pain and frustration.
>
> Reaching a point where I felt I couldn't go on, I called some Christians I'd met years before and they invited me to their church. I was a typical hippie—no shoes and no bra—but I went to the altar that night and prayed, "Lord, if you will just forgive me, I'll serve you the rest of my life."
>
> As I lifted my hands to worship him I felt the Lord was saying, "Marie, I've already forgiven you. I see you the way you want me to see you, and I love you."
>
> From that day on, I tried to live a godly life. I dropped out of college because I feared my ungodly friends and bad habits would pull me back down.
>
> Attending church regularly, I soon met Mike. His Christian family, with loving relationships and many happy traditions, was everything my own family was not. When Mike and I were married later that year his family accepted me and tried to love me, but I really didn't know how to receive their love. Being around them only reminded me of my own dysfunctional family.
>
> What I really wanted was for my own dad, my own stepmother, to love me as Mike's family loved him. But Dad had

practically disowned me because I had married a simple man—not someone wealthy and prominent—and I had married outside his church. I felt I could never be completely happy, even though we had lots of friends, Mike had a good job, and we had a beautiful home.

Marie tried to focus on the positive and put all of life's negatives behind her as she quoted, "Old things have passed away; behold, all things have become new" (2 Cor 5:17b, NKJV). But it seemed she had a broken area deep inside her that all the memorized Scriptures never touched, and that she dared not reveal to her friends. Then there was the happy exterior—the smiling Marie everybody knew. No doubt many Christians today find themselves in these same circumstances. "I even counseled and prayed with people and had them say, 'Oh, you've helped me so much!'" Marie reported. "Yet my pain never went away."

MISSIONARY WITH A BROKEN HEART

After they had two children, she and Mike felt called to missions work. Before long they moved to Mexico to help operate a training program. "I'm going to forget about these feelings deep inside me, find my joy in Jesus, and serve him with everything I have," Marie determined.

She immersed herself in the needs of the people with broken homes and other hurts, her happy facade firmly in place. But eventually she came to the end of herself and began crying out to God for wholeness. Then someone mailed her a copy of our book, *A Woman's Guide to Spiritual Warfare*, and she read about the freedom that comes with forgiving. Marie reported:

> I'd always said that I forgave my father, but I knew God was telling me to deal with my feelings on a deeper level. In prayer I went back to the time before he had rejected me. I said, "Lord,

you knew that my parents, Richard and Margaret, would come together in love, and you chose to give life to that seed so that I would be born. You didn't cause all the abuse I suffered. My parents didn't know better, but you knew that I would have joy in the end."

I realized that without Jesus, my behavior was no better than theirs. Then I began to feel real love and compassion for my father—a confused man who didn't know what to do or how to cope with his baby daughter. I saw Darlene's frustration with her barrenness, and realized her beating me was simply her way of dealing with that. Had she been a whole person, she could have found joy in loving me.

As Marie allowed the Holy Spirit to help her see her circumstances from God's point of view, she was able truly to forgive her father and stepmother, and her healing began. She also forgave her birth mother, Margaret, for abandoning her—although she's had no direct contact with her and has no idea where she is. Then she forgave her new stepmother, who seemed to cause an even greater rift between Marie and her father.

From a heart filled with Christ's love for her parents, Marie prayed that God's mercy and compassion would touch and change their lives. And she prayed that God would give her father a natural affection for her, his only child.

Only three days later Marie received a letter from her dad, written on the same day she had prayed her prayer of forgiveness. It had been mailed to a Texas border town, then brought across to Mexico by one of her coworkers. The note read, "Dear Marie, here's a check. I was thinking about you today… thought you might need some money to get home."

"I know it doesn't sound like much," Marie said, "but in our three years in Mexico, he had shown no interest in me at all. He was angry that I'd brought his grandchildren here, and said he would never come to see us.

"A few months after the letter I went home to test the miracle.

The Lord said, 'Marie, I want you to esteem him as your father.' Before this change in me came about I was terrified of my father, but the Lord helped me find something I could be proud of. I looked him in the eye and said, 'Dad, I'm so proud of you. You're a banker, and I read in the news all the time about bankers being dishonest. But you've had millions of dollars go through your hands, and you've always been honest.' I realized I could say that because I had forgiven him."

At her words, he seemed to melt.

"'Marie, I'm proud of you too,' Richard replied, 'and you're always welcome to come here. I appreciate the way you're raising your kids—you're doing a good job. I love you and I want you to take care of yourself.'

"In all my thirty-four years I had never heard such words from my father. They were greater than gold. At last I had received the miracle of my dad's love and his blessing. It was the beginning of a new life for me."

HEALING LOVE

Marie says the only thing that healed her was Jesus' love for the people who had hurt her. Yet for that love to be released, she had to forgive them. "The power of forgiveness is so strong," she concluded. "I believe that's why Jesus said on the cross, 'Father, forgive them, for they do not know what they are doing' (Lk 23:34a). He wanted that power to go forth."

Marie's experience is an example of how a person may truly love God and sincerely try to be a good Christian, yet hidden hurts from the past keep her in a bondage of pain she can't even describe. We counsel and pray with women in similar situations every week. If you are crying out to God for help as Marie was, be assured that he hears you and that help is on the way. The Holy Spirit is always faithful to reveal, at the proper time, the areas where forgiveness is needed. As you submit to his guidance, the Lord will enable you to obey what he asks you to do.

EMOTIONAL DEPENDENCY

Esther is a friend who struggled for more than ten years with the bondage of an illicit relationship with a minister and the bitterness it produced in her before she broke through to freedom.

"I knew my behavior was wrong, and I repeatedly repented afterward, but I was emotionally dependent upon this man," Esther told us. "I came out of the counterculture when I accepted Christ, and a short time later fell in love with Robert, a dynamic young minister. Flattered by his attention, I yielded to his sexual advances, just as I had done with boyfriends during my hippie days."

Esther and Robert often talked about getting married. But this dream for the future served only to keep her in the relationship. For Robert, their talks seemed to be his way of justifying the sin.

"I'd convince myself that once we got married we'd be exonerated from our sin," Esther said. "Yet deep in my heart I knew that wasn't true. Because of our sexual union the bond was very strong, and I seemed powerless to get out of the relationship. Robert had other girlfriends at various times while he was dating me, but I naïvely thought I would win out over them. I had allowed the enemy to deceive me because I so desperately wanted this relationship to work."

Esther became increasingly unhappy and guilt-ridden as the years went by with no wedding plans in the making. The turning point came while she was visiting an aunt in a distant city and went with her to a Bible study.

The teacher, a pastor in the liturgical denomination Esther had been reared in, talked about the power of confession. Though she never had understood the gospel during her growing-up years in the church, she was familiar with the tradition of confession. Suddenly she felt she could talk to this pastor about the weight of guilt she was carrying. Because he knew no one in her circle of friends, it would be safe.

"Being honest with another person and confessing my sin is

what broke the bondage," Esther shared. "In some ways Robert had taken advantage of me, yet I had to confess that I, too, was a participant in the sin. Over the next year I had several counseling sessions with this pastor, and I became accountable to him. He helped me to face reality and to ask hard questions about this relationship."

When Esther told Robert she had confessed to a pastor and was receiving counseling, he was angry—partly because he feared exposure, partly because he disagreed theologically with the concept of confession. In the end, they decided to break up.

Next, Esther faced the challenge of forgiving Robert for the disappointment, the wasted years, her feelings of betrayal.

> I searched the Scriptures and asked the Lord to help me. The miracle is that he gave me a strategy for forgiveness through Matthew 18:21-22:
>
> "Then Peter came to Him and said, 'Lord, how often shall my brother sin against me, and I forgive him? Up to seven times?' Jesus said to him, 'I do not say to you, up to seven times, but up to seventy times seven'" (NKJV).
>
> I asked the Lord what that means, and he said, "Every time you think of it." He showed me I couldn't do it all at once—it was a process.
>
> For about six months I had flashbacks of events from our relationship, but the Lord helped me to forgive each memory. Every time I thought of something Robert had done to disappoint me, I would forgive him.

But Esther still had a forgiveness problem: to forgive herself.

"After I'd forgiven Robert, I had flashbacks which focused more on me—my sinfulness, rebellion, and disobedience," she says. "Again, with every memory I would confess, repent of my sin, and receive God's forgiveness. Over the next six months I was able to put regret behind me. Within a year I was free from the bondage of the relationship."

Was she frustrated about still being single? "Once I was free of guilt and no longer felt trapped, I began learning to have healthy friendships," she reports.

"Because I had to keep the sinful parts of my relationship with Robert from them, I couldn't be completely open with any of my friends. But when I obeyed the Lord and began to walk in purity, I regained my self-esteem. I was content with my single life for several years, and now am happily married to a wonderful Christian man. I am so grateful that God forgives and forgets the past!"

FORGIVENESS AND "LETTING GO"

As Esther and many others we've talked to have discovered, forgiveness is not a onetime choice; it is ongoing and progressive. You deal with one layer at a time. Why, in her case, did more than ten years go by before the situation was resolved? Perhaps it took that long for Esther to want God's peace strongly enough to let go of an unhealthy relationship.

Dr. H. Norman Wright, in discussing the importance of a daughter forgiving her father, gives this graphic picture:

> Forgiveness involves letting go. Remember playing tug-of-war as a child? As long as the parties on each end of the rope are tugging, you have a "war." But when someone lets go, the war is over. When you forgive your father, you are letting go of your end of the rope. No matter how hard he may tug on the other end, if you have released your end, the war is over for you.[1]

God deals with each of his children on an individual basis in this process of forgiving. He always does it in love. But it is the major key to walking free from bondage.

PRAYER

Lord, I truly mean it when I pray, "Forgive us our debts, as we also have forgiven our debtors" (Mt 6:12). Thank you for helping me work my way through the process of forgiving those who have wounded me.

Thank you for the mercy you have shown by forgiving all my sins. Please, Lord, help me to show mercy to others. Help me to choose to forgive each time a painful memory comes back, or whenever someone offends me. I rejoice in the freedom forgiveness brings to my life! Amen.

FIFTEEN

Developing Spiritual Discernment

We know also that the Son of God has come and has given us understanding, so that we may know him who is true. **1 John 5:20a**

Discernment is our safeguard against deception! Since women tend to be more sensitive to the spiritual realm than men, they make good prayer warriors. What mother hasn't, at one time or another, felt her child was in danger and in need of her prayers? Her spiritual antenna picked up the warning.

But ever since the Garden of Eden women have also had to guard against deception. The crafty devil will whisper in our ears as his did in Eve's, "Indeed, has God said... ?"

We need a radar system that flashes, "WARNING, enemy at work!"

MILITARY STRATEGY

One of the most strategic military defense installations in the world is hidden in a Colorado mountain I (Quin) can see from my upstairs home office window. This mountain conceals a vast complex of underground chambers comprising the North American Air Defense Command (NORAD), an early warning system that can track strategic enemy missile activity anywhere on this globe.

As Christians, we need to function like an early warning radar installation, as spiritual NORADs, to discern where the enemy is attacking, what his strategies are, and then what action to take to stop those tactics.

Sometimes we are called to defend someone close to us. Other times, the Holy Spirit calls upon us to pray for people we don't even know—national leaders and public figures, pastors and spiritual leaders, or specific nations of the world. We must be alert, listening for the Holy Spirit's voice, and ever aware of the enemy. Yet we must be even more aware of our help. Not trusting in a mountain, but in the God of the mountain. We can say with the psalmist: "I lift up my eyes to the hills—where does my help come from? My help comes from the Lord, the Maker of heaven and earth" (Ps 121:1-2).

HOW DO WE DISCERN VOICES?

Paul prayed this prayer for the believers at Philippi: "... that your love may abound more and more in knowledge and depth of insight, so that you may be able to discern what is best and may be pure and blameless until the day of Christ" (Phil 1:9-10). This is a prayer model for others as well as for ourselves.

How do we become discerning believers? Author and teacher Tom White explains:

> General discernment is an endowment of the Holy Spirit to every believer, enabling him or her to perceive personally the grace of God which is available to help the person become holy and avoid evil. The purpose of discernment is to see what God has for us, and to walk in it.[1]

As we ask God for direction and await his response, we must discern between three possible voices: our own, God's, or Satan's.

We produce the majority of our thoughts ourselves. For example, we make plans for ourselves and our families, think through solutions to problems, draw conclusions based on our knowledge of a situation, etc. But often our knowledge is incomplete, our thinking flawed, and thus we're susceptible to error and deception.

Other thoughts can come from God; the Creator can speak into our minds with a spark of revelation or an inner voice, by the gift of a word of knowledge, through Scripture verses, songs, sermons, or devotional readings. God can speak in any way he chooses.

The third possible source of a thought is our enemy. Satan and his representatives seek to influence us by planting thoughts in our minds contrary to God's Word or purpose. Remember that God will convict you for wrongdoing or wrong attitudes and call you to repentance. But the devil always condemns you when you fail, burdening you with guilt, and making you feel hopeless and unworthy of forgiveness. Be quick to discern the difference. The instant you recognize the enemy's voice, immediately resist him and silence him.

Once when I (Ruthanne) was praying for a loved one I suddenly recognized the voice of the enemy. "What makes you think praying will help?" the voice taunted. "He'll never change!"

For a moment I abruptly stopped praying, surprised by this interruption. Then I addressed the enemy: "Satan, I command you to be silent—you have no authority to speak to me. I resist you and refuse to hear your voice, in Jesus' name. I declare that I have the mind of Christ (1 Cor 2:16) and that my prayer is according to the will of God."

Bible teacher Dean Sherman explains:

> When the Scriptures speak of Satan or the devil, sometimes they are referring to his evil empire rather than the individual, Lucifer himself. The devil couldn't possibly be in hundreds of thousands of places at the same time, tempting people and

> putting suggestions in their minds. His fallen angels are the ones carrying out Satan's orders.... When God's Word tells us to resist the devil, I believe it is telling us to resist spirit beings belonging to Lucifer.
>
> ... While the forces of darkness cannot read our minds—only God can do that (Ps 7:9)—they can put suggestions there.... Most spiritual warfare takes place in the human mind.[2]

As Sherman points out, we need to recognize when a thought does not agree with God's truth. The enemy enjoys discrediting people and destroying relationships. He delights to fill our thoughts with accusations against ourselves and others. He is both "the father of lies" (Jn 8:44) and the "accuser of the brethren" (Rv 12:10).

But God is a loving Father. When we pray and ask him for guidance we can be certain of two things:

1. His answer or direction to us will not be contrary to his Word as recorded in the Bible.
2. It will not be contrary to his character.

For example, it goes against God's Word and his character to tell a woman she should murder a doctor who performs abortions, or that she should attack a person who abused her child. Therefore if someone justifies such action by saying, "God told me to do it," you know she heeded an alien voice—it could not have been God's voice.

God gave directions for discerning the voices of spirits:

> Dear friends, do not believe every spirit, but test the spirits to see whether they are from God, because many false prophets have gone out into the world. This is how you recognize the Spirit of God: Every spirit that acknowledges that Jesus Christ has come in the flesh is from God, but every spirit that does not acknowledge Jesus is not from God. This is the spirit of the antichrist.
>
> **1 John 4:1-3a**

Jesus himself warned his followers: "Watch out that you are not deceived" (Lk 21:8a).

HONORING GOD IN OUR HOMES

We honor God in our homes by removing anything from them that represents the kingdom of darkness. Tom White explains:

> Evil spirits can pollute places with their unholy presence. Such demonization usually occurs when mortal beings commit immoral acts that open the door to the activity of demons. For example, a house used for the manufacture or selling of drugs, a place used for prostitution, or a building used by a fortune-teller or spiritualist group may invite demons of bondage, deception, violence, lust, sexual perversion or familiar spirits of the occult. Even when the perpetrators have left the scene, evil spirits may linger, hoping to prey upon unsuspecting newcomers.[3]

Scripture declares, "Do not bring a detestable thing into your house or you, like it, will be set apart for destruction. Utterly abhor and detest it, for it is set apart for destruction" (Dt 7:26). Many Christians reject this verse, saying that because it's part of the Old Testament it doesn't apply to us today. On the other hand, why would a believer who seeks to serve the Lord with all her heart want to have in her possession objects which represent the enemy?

Consider again our example of the refugee in chapter one. Can you imagine that person, after a miraculous escape to freedom, keeping a portrait on her dresser of the cruel dictator from whom she'd just been delivered?

One of our Christian readers wrote to us about a Chinese antique she had inherited from her mother. She described the piece as a decorative screen covered with dragons, and added that since she had placed the antique in her bedroom she had started waking up frequently during the night. She felt uneasy when she prayed about what to do with the screen, and she wondered whether she should get rid of it.

We pointed out that dragons represent Satan in several biblical passages, then asked her, "Do you think the screen in your home brings glory to God?" We told her to go back to prayer and let God give her the answer.

A few months later she wrote back, saying she had gotten rid of the screen. She reported with surprise that as soon as she got it out of her bedroom, she was no longer bothered by insomnia. Only then did she remember that her own mother had begun to suffer with insomnia about the time she had inherited the family heirloom.

This incident may strike you as being rather bizarre, but we could cite many such examples from readers and women who've attended our teaching sessions in many countries of the world.

We don't mean to imply that every physical problem you encounter can be attributed to a supernatural, evil cause. Nor can we supply you with an exhaustive list of objects you need to remove from your home. Some items are blatantly occult while others appear to be harmless. But because of the prior use of some items, or painful experiences associated with them, the Holy Spirit may prompt you to dispose of them. The point is, you yourself must seek the Lord and get direction in the matter. The Word of God and the counsel of other believers are your safeguards against being deceived.

KNOWING GOD'S VOICE

For many believers, the idea of asking God for guidance, then discerning his response, is a scary proposition. They don't feel capable of hearing from God. Isn't it only super-spiritual people who can do that?

That's exactly what the enemy wants you to think. It keeps you from doing damage to his territory. Or it keeps you running from place to place, hoping to "get a word from God" through somebody else.

Any person willing to spend the time in worship, prayer, medi-tation, and Bible reading can hear from God. He is our shepherd, and he gives us this promise:

> He calls his own sheep by name and leads them out. When he has brought out all his own, he goes on ahead of them, and his sheep follow him because they know his voice. But they will never follow a stranger; in fact, they will run away from him because they do not recognize a stranger's voice. **John 10:3b-5**

We learn to recognize God's voice by staying close to him as a sheep stays close to his shepherd. If you're a wounded sheep, you stay especially close and allow him to heal you. For periods of time the shepherd may even carry you—but he can't do that if you run away. The closer you are to the shepherd the more familiar his voice becomes, and the more you prefer it above the noise of the world.

Recognizing the voice of an imposter is not so difficult when you truly know your shepherd's voice. You will refuse to listen to the voice of the enemy, or to your own voice of selfishness or human reasoning. Never negotiate with the enemy or entertain his suggestions!

Solomon asked God for a discerning heart to distinguish between right and wrong. Here, then, is the key: Ask God for discernment. God was pleased with Solomon's request and honored it (see 1 Kings 3:9-12).

"God gave Solomon wisdom and *very great discernment* and breadth of mind, like the sand that is on the seashore" (1 Kgs 4:29, NASB, italics mine). Another translation calls it "very great insight, and a breadth of understanding" (NIV). This is a Scripture I (Quin) prayed for my children when they were in college.

On one occasion, recorded in the Book of Samuel, David was spared from committing murder because Abigail acted on her discernment and averted the crisis. Her husband, Nabal, had refused to feed David and his men even after they had protected his flocks. In his anger David intended to wipe out Nabal's entire household. But Abigail "headed him off at the pass," you might say. She

supplies onto several donkeys, took them to David
en, and appealed to him not to shed blood.

nswered, "Blessed be the Lord God of Israel, who sent you
ay to meet me, and blessed be your discernment, and blessed
you, who have kept me this day from bloodshed, and from
avenging myself by my own hand" (1 Sm 25:32b-33, NASB).

SUGGESTIONS FOR DISCERNMENT

Several godly women counselors gave the following responses when asked how they learned to be discerning for themselves or about others:

- My rule of thumb is, "Don't doubt your doubts." If your first response was a red flag, don't talk yourself out of it.
- If I sense a "red flag," I stop and move with caution. It's like a radar warning.
- I watch for incongruities in people's behavior.
- Sometimes I detect an uncleanness—not physically, but spiritually, usually by studying their eyes or their body language.
- God just seems to give me intuition when I need it; it's actually the Holy Spirit's promptings.
- When I ask him for wisdom and understanding I expect to receive from him; sometimes he drops pictures or words into my mind.

Seek confirmation. In a situation where you're emotionally involved, it's more difficult to discern situations clearly, because your own human desires in the matter easily cloud your perception. *The objective input of an outside friend or prayer partner can protect you from extremes.*

Again a warning is needed: be careful not to take personal prophecy as direct guidance. Usually God has already spoken to you about a matter, and a prophetic word should confirm what you're already sensing as God's direction. If you receive a word that's a puzzle to you, just put it aside, pray about it, but don't try to make it happen. If it is from God, he will bring it to pass in his timing.

I (Quin) remember a time when a minister called me up after a meeting and told me the Lord had shown her that I would write many books and they would be translated into various languages. This came at a time of great discouragement in my life; I'd just nursed Mother through cancer until her death and had not been able to write in over a year. But sure enough, within the next eighteen months I finished my first book and it is now in eight languages. But when I received the prophetic word, I simply "filed it away" without dwelling on it. "God, if that is you I trust you to bring it to pass," I'd said the night I heard it.

Listen to your "radar." A number of readers have written us about missing the direction of the Holy Spirit when they should have heard his warnings.

One Christian woman wrote to us, "The disaster of my life came when a classmate became a good friend of mine. Something inside me was telling me not to trust her. However, my kind heart ignored all the signals. I became very close to her, and introduced her to my husband. Now my husband admits to being in love with her."

That "something inside" telling her not to trust this other woman was her "radar"—the Holy Spirit's early warning system. Now she wishes she had heeded it.

Many readers have asked for prayer and direction concerning their finances. This is an area where women often have poor discernment; thus the enemy has gotten many into bondage. We advocate that you pay tithes and seek God for wisdom in being a good steward of his provision for you. If your husband refuses to pay tithes on his income, you are not responsible. (See our chapter on "Material Provision" in *The Spiritual Warrior's Prayer Guide*.) The goal is not just to get out of debt. The important thing is to seek to know God and his Word better, to obey him, and to get clear discernment in order to avoid such bondages in the future.

Discerning evil activity. The enemy works actively to destroy individuals, families, churches, and whole communities. Pornography is one of his destructive tools.

Mary Jane and some of her prayer partners discerned evil activity in their community and were particularly concerned when a nude nightclub began to hire high school girls. This group of women drove to the site in the daytime to pray and do spiritual warfare.

"We prayed the Word of God as we drove around that building," Mary Jane reported. "We believed our warfare prayers had really paid off when we saw the nude nightclub closed down!"

However, the very next day an X-rated bookstore and video shop opened up. At first, they were really surprised, and then realized the Lord was teaching them a lesson.

"We now know we should have prayed for the building to fall into the hands of Christians. We went to battle again, concerned about how many families were affected by that store. We believe people getting materials from there were taking evil spirits home to their families, exposing them to the horrors of pornography.

"We fasted, asked for discernment, and prayed the Word of God. The Lord gave us strategy. We asked God to keep customers away when we were driving around the building. After doing this over a period of time, one day several of us went into the store (as though we were customers) for six minutes of prayer. We laid hands on those videos and books and commanded the fruit of them to wither and die. We prayed the building would be occupied by Christians who would use it for righteous purposes."

Soon they read in the newspaper that a used car business was opening there, and to their delight they recognized the owner's name—a Christian businessman. The article said the owners of the adult video and book store were not able to pay their rent; they closed because their business was not profitable. A direct answer to prayer!

Dreams and visions. God speaks to us in many ways. One of the ways he's used since the beginning of time has been through dreams and visions; dreams occur while we sleep, and visions while we are awake.

Herman Riffel, a minister who has studied the topic intensively, suggests four ways to check the interpretation of your dreams:

1. Go directly to God in prayer for confirmation, remembering that God speaks to us in different ways, dreams being only one of them.
2. Check Scripture, since God doesn't contradict Himself by saying one thing in the Bible and the opposite in a dream.
3. Seek confirmation from trusted friends and associates.
4. Heed the feeling you have in your own spirit about the interpretation. Even if you don't like the message, the truth of it will usually plant itself in your heart.[4]

God provides us with an "Early Warning System" with his gift of discernment through the Holy Spirit. If we pay attention to the signals and obey his directions, we can avoid a lot of enemy fire. And we can help others get free from bondage.

PRAYER

Father, I ask for your discernment. I need it, I long for it. I don't want to be deceived. Along with discernment I ask for wisdom, understanding, and knowledge. Let me learn to distinguish your still, small voice from all the other voices vying for my attention and action.

Lord, may your sweet Holy Spirit be so real to me that I will yield to his direction and guidance. Lord, I need your supernatural touch on my life. Give me a fresh anointing of discernment. Thank you, precious Lord. Amen.

SIXTEEN

Helping Family and Friends Break Free

Be on the alert. Your adversary, the devil, prowls about like a roaring lion, seeking someone to devour. But resist him, firm in your faith.

1 Peter 5:8b, 9a NASB

Maybe you can identify with heartaches similar to those our readers have shared with us, wanting prayer and guidance concerning how to break bondages plaguing their loved ones:

- We received a phone bill of $447 for calls made to an adult talk number by our fifteen-year-old son; we've just discovered he's into pornographic magazines and videos.
- Satan has brought strife between my mother and my husband, and since we live with Mom I don't know who to side with. I'm really depressed about it all.
- My son has been in a hospital for abusing prescription drugs.
- My divorced daughter is very rebellious and stubborn. I am afraid her boyfriend is molesting her little daughter, but she won't listen to me.
- My husband keeps having one affair after another, but he still lives with me.

WARFARE PRAYER

We know clearly from the apostle Paul's teaching on spiritual warfare that our struggle is not against flesh and blood—our husbands, children, relatives, or friends—but against rulers, authorities, powers of this dark world, spiritual forces of evil in the heavenly realms (see Ephesians 6:12). In other words, Satan has a hierarchy of demonic forces that carry out his plans and orders to promote a kingdom of evil. It's clear that our warfare is against invisible powers who have different levels of authority.

We strongly agree with Dr. C. Peter Wagner, Fuller Theological Seminary professor, who has studied and written much on Satan's strategy, when he writes:

> Satan's central task and desire is to prevent God from being glorified...
>
> a. by keeping lost people from being saved...
>
> b. by making human beings and human society as miserable as possible in this present life.
>
> The enemy has come to steal, to kill and to destroy. When we see wars, poverty, oppression, sickness, racism, greed and similar evils too numerous to list, we have no doubt that Satan is succeeding all too much. None of these things bring glory to God. But these are secondary objectives because each is only a temporal victory.[1]

Dr. Wagner reminds us that Satan has accumulated millennia of experience at blinding people and preventing them from believing the gospel. Obviously the apostle Paul understood this tactic of the enemy when he wrote: "The god of this age has blinded the minds of unbelievers, so that they cannot see the light of the gospel of the glory of Christ, who is the image of God" (2 Cor 4:4).

Seeing those we love in such great bondages, we yearn to set them free. One of the keys God has given us is intercession.

What exactly is intercession? It means to "stand between or to mediate between two people." It's prayer! When you and I intercede for another person, we stand in the gap between God and that person, beseeching God on his behalf. We also stand between Satan and that person, battling for his or her release. One Bible teacher describes "gap" as the distance between where something is and where God wants it to be.

Our intercession restricts satanic forces and allows the Holy Spirit to open the unbeliever's eyes and bring conviction, repentance, and godly change in the life of the one for whom we pray.

To engage in warfare prayer we must be certain that we're wearing the full armor God provides (see our discussion of this in our book *The Spiritual Warrior's Prayer Guide*). Paul tells us that in addition to being clothed in God's armor, we are to "pray in the Spirit on all occasions with all kinds of prayers and requests... be alert and always keep on praying for all the saints" (Eph 6:18).

OUR SPIRITUAL WEAPONS

Jesus told his followers (and that includes us): "I have given you authority to trample on snakes and scorpions, and to overcome all the power of the enemy.... However, do not rejoice that the spirits submit to you, but rejoice that your names are written in heaven" (Lk 10:19-20).

That means our Lord has empowered us with his authority! What do we do with it? Use it against the enemy! We have received hundreds of letters from readers of our previous books who tell us they never realized before that they had authority to stand against Satan's onslaughts on their families.

But having been invested with Christ's authority, we now have a responsibility to keep an intimate relationship with him through prayer. And to heed this instruction: "Do your best to present yourself to God as one approved, a workman who does not need to be ashamed and who correctly handles the word of truth" (2 Tm 2:15).

Word of God is called the sword of the Spirit, and it is our ary weapon in warfare (see Ephesians 6:17 and Hebrews 2). But you must become acquainted with Scripture as a whole—not just grabbing a verse like you would a fire extinguisher to deal with an emergency, then putting it away again.

I (Quin) have a plan that I use in my devotional time called the four W's: Worship. Wait. Word. Warfare. I worship the Lord, then wait for him to show me from his Word what Scriptures to use in warfare. This is not a pat formula, but a way of praying that works for me.

Binding and loosing is another tactic the Scripture provides for coming against demonic forces holding our loved ones in captivity. As Jesus declared to Peter: "I will give you the keys of the kingdom of heaven; whatever you bind on earth will be bound in heaven, and whatever you loose on earth will be loosed in heaven" (Mt 16:19).

The *Spirit Filled Life Bible* commentary states:

> [In this verse] Jesus is passing on to His church His authority or control to bind and to loose on earth. The Greek construction behind ***will be bound*** and ***will be loosed*** indicates that Jesus is the One who has activated the provisions through His Cross; the church is then charged with implementation of what He has released through His life, death, and resurrection.... Clearly rabbinic in imagery, binding and loosing have to do with forbidding or permitting.[2]

Another explanation:

> To bind is to secure the enemy with pressure so he cannot move. To loose is to gain liberty using the Word of God. Binding refers to the enemy, while loosing refers to the victory.... There is no formula for binding and loosing; it must be done by revelation of His Spirit.[3]

Other Scriptures give added strength to the activity of binding the enemy, which is actually forbidding his continued onslaught. For instance, Jesus said, "How can one enter a strong man's house and plunder his goods, unless he firsts binds the strong man? And then he will plunder his house" (Mt 12:29, NKJV; also see Luke 11:21-22).

BINDING DEMONIC SPIRITS

Belle, a Christian woman, lived with an abusive husband almost forty years before he died of an alcohol-related disease. Jim controlled his drinking so that it didn't interfere with his job, but when he came home in the evenings, he'd drink until he passed out in his chair. He often yelled at his family; other times he physically abused the children. Belle recalls:

> One night Jim sat on the front steps of our house waiting for our oldest son to return home because he believed our son had stolen fifty cents from him. Jim was armed with a huge knife that he had brought home after the war, a weapon used by the warlike Gurkhas of Nepal. I sat at the top of the steps binding the demons and crying out to the Lord for help. Soon Jim dropped the knife and came to bed.
>
> Often when I sat with him while he was drunk, I would whisper under my breath to bind the demons. Sometimes Jim would say, "Don't talk to me like that."
>
> I would reply, "I didn't say anything to you—I didn't speak aloud." He'd give me a puzzled look.

Belle told us that no one taught her about binding and loosing—she just saw it in the Word of God one day when she was desperate to keep Jim from harming the children. She began asking the Lord which spirits were operating through Jim during his alcoholic bouts, like anger, murder, violence, and lies. Her binding these spirits prevented him from wounding her or the children.

"Jim surrendered himself fully to our Lord just before his death, so all my years of praying for him paid off," she concluded. You would have a hard time convincing Belle that spiritual warfare doesn't work!

THE HOLY SPIRIT, OUR HELPER

Before Jesus went to heaven he promised his followers, "I will ask the Father, and He will give you another Comforter (Counselor, Helper, Intercessor, Advocate, Strengthener, and Standby) that He may remain with you forever, the Spirit of Truth... He will teach you all things" (Jn 14:16-17a, 26b, AMPLIFIED).

The apostle Paul teaches that when Christians allow the Holy Spirit to pray through them, they are praying according to God's will. Some Christians interpret "according to God's will" to mean that through Bible study and prayer they will discern his will, and then pray it accordingly.

Others believe the Holy Spirit intercedes through them when they pray in tongues. When we don't know how to pray, we can allow the Holy Spirit to pray through us in languages we haven't learned, as these verses explain:

> In the same way, the Spirit helps us in our weakness. We do not know what we ought to pray for, but the Spirit himself intercedes for us with groans that words cannot express. And he who searches our hearts knows the mind of the Spirit, because the Spirit intercedes for the saints in accordance with God's will.
>
> **Romans 8:26-27**

> For anyone who speaks in a tongue does not speak to men but to God.... I would like every one of you to speak in tongues....
>
> **1 Corinthians 14:2a, 5a**

Author and pastor Judson Cornwall says, "Prayer is the most valuable use of tongues for it is 'speaking to God.'" He goes on to explain:

> ... The Holy Spirit is certainly not limited to the English language nor is He confined to modern languages. He has access to every language ever used by mankind, and He is very familiar with the language used in heaven. When deep intercession is needed, the Spirit often uses a language that is beyond the intellectual grasp of the speaker to bypass the censorship of his or her conscious mind, thereby enabling the Spirit to say what needs to be prayed without arguing with the faith level of the one through whom the intercession flows.... Intercessory prayer in tongues is not incoherent speech. The very words are motivated by the Holy Spirit, addressed to the Father and approved by the Lord Jesus (see Mark 16:1).... The language is spoken with complete cooperation of the praying person.[4]

This gift of unknown tongues is available to all born-again Christians, not just those who lived in the first-century church. As a child of God, all you need to do is ask (see Luke 11:11-13).

SPIRITUAL WARFARE FOR MOTHERS

Mothers are often the prime intercessors for their children. We need to be prepared to do battle on their behalf.

Nona is such a mom. Her daughter Lorene, who has a slight learning disability, began to behave in a peculiar manner when she turned fourteen.

"She'd switch from being a little girl who loved to talk to her teddy bears and dolls to an adult personality with a flippant attitude and a deep voice—all within a few hours," Nona reported. "She would put on far too much makeup and act so strangely, it was hard to believe she was my same sweet little girl. She began to hear voices saying, 'Satan is God. God is Satan,' and fly into angry rages."

Nona, a single mother with five children, was a new Christian with no experience in spiritual warfare. She sought out a pastor known for a deliverance ministry to pray for Lorene. Not only did he pray over her daughter, he also cast out a spirit of anger that left her immediately.

The pastor gave Nona several tools to use in her daughter's healing: On a cassette tape he recorded a prayer for her and instructed Nona to play it for Lorene several times a day. She was to get rid of any ungodly music tapes, and instead flood the room with Christian music—tapes of Scripture choruses and hymns.

He also gave Nona a written prayer to pray aloud twice a day as she soaked her daughter in prayer. This was not a "magic formula" or incantation, but a declaration of her trust in God for Lorene's healing.

The other personality changes were dealt with at home by Nona herself praying and taking authority over evil influences in her daughter. Lorene sometimes was cooperative, at other times she was resistant. When the child doesn't cooperate, a mother can still play a decisive role in seeing her child set free by praying and doing warfare even when the child is not present. She can also bind the spirits operating through a rebellious child and hinder their activity. Nona says Lorene's recovery was a progressive one, but after about a year her daughter was back to her normal sweet self.

We caution you that when you see personality changes in a loved one, professional help is usually needed. Do not assume that a demonic deliverance will provide a "quick fix." If deliverance is the key, that person will still need proper follow-up and discipling. But we do encourage you to blanket that person with prayer and praise while they receive whatever professional help may be needed.

One woman told us of her thirty-seven-year-old son's five-year battle with AIDS and the decision she and her husband made to stand in the gap for him. Dixie and Frank allowed their son

Donald to move into their backyard cottage when he could no longer hold a full-time job.

As his condition deteriorated, he began taking high-powered drugs. With the drug use, tormenting and harassing spirits began to manifest themselves through Donald as he raged angrily against his parents.

"I have come to realize that when Donald calls us names, writes us poison letters, and smashes our prized possessions, this is actually the demons working through him," says Dixie. "He has a free will that has chosen not to accept Jesus—at least not yet—so the medications make him vulnerable to this demonic activity."

When these episodes began, Dixie, Frank, and their prayer partner began speaking to the spirits tormenting her son: "We bind all spirits operating through Donald and command you to be silent. We use the authority and power of the name and blood of Jesus Christ to declare that our son will be loosed from demonic powers."

After they'd battled like this for several days, Donald called near midnight one Sunday asking his dad to forgive him with tears of remorse. He also wanted to speak to Dixie, to beg her forgiveness, but she asked him to come the next day in person.

"I wanted eye contact, in case those demons in him started acting up," Dixie reported. "Also, I needed to be sure he was sincere. And I wanted to put my arms around him and love him—not just have him hear me say, 'I forgive you' in an impersonal telephone conversation. We are beginning to see a breakthrough at last. He is truly sorry he went on a rampage. It was like seeing a tiny ray of light at the end of what's been a long dark tunnel."

Dixie has been a praying mother for years. She says, "As mothers we are sensitive to see into the spiritual realm, and that helps us know how to pray more effectively. Naturally, as mothers, we want to 'fix' our children's problems. But I can't fix Donald's life. I will no longer come to his rescue—financially, medically, or in any other way. But I will battle in the heavenly realm against the demonic spirits tormenting my son and blinding him to the truth about Jesus, his Savior."

Donald has bleeding sores. His skin grafts haven't taken, and, barring a miracle, he faces imminent death. His sexual partner has already died—but he accepted Jesus a few weeks before he did. Dixie believes Donald will soon accept the Lord.

Three times a week Dixie and her prayer partner meet for three-hour prayer sessions. "When we pray for Donald, we ask the Father what is on his heart for us to pray. And since I'm counseling other relatives of AIDS patients, we pray for them too." Her prayer strategy changes from week to week, but these are guidelines she often follows:

1. She claims the blessings from Deuteronomy 28 for her son and their entire household and comes against curses mentioned.
2. She claims for her son Galatians 3:13a, "Christ redeemed us from the curse of the law by becoming a curse for us."
3. The Scripture "Believe in the Lord Jesus, and you will be saved—you and your household" has been a promise she's clung to a long time (see Acts 16:31). She believes it for her gay son.
4. She speaks the peace of the Lord over all the confusion and torment her son is undergoing both from pain in his body and torment to his mind.
5. The Lord convicted her to forgive Donald and release him from her judgment. She no longer mumbles and complains about anything he has done to hurt and wound her, but is grateful for the happy years they've had.
6. The Lord is allowing her to work with support groups to help others going through the pain of seeing loved ones suffer from AIDS.
7. She actively prays against the influences that come through other people—his gay friends, people he meets in the secular psychiatrist's office, etc. "Lord, guard him from wrong influences."

A GRANDMOTHER'S BATTLE

The story that follows lacks a victorious ending, but will encourage you to ask the Lord for strategy when engaged in spiritual combat.

Maria is a grandmother denied the right to see her grandchildren, a heartache with which many readers can identify.

Maria fights in the spiritual realm for the release of her daughter Candace—a virtual prisoner in her own home. "She's been brainwashed by a demanding husband who quotes Scripture to keep her in submission," she told Quin. "Candace runs a small business out of their home, a home which is in such disrepair it doesn't even have a functioning sink. While she's working, her husband Chuck hangs out at the beach."

Once Chuck beat Candace so badly she had to go to a home for abused women until her wounds had healed. The counselors advised her to find a "safe house" for at least six months. She went to stay with her mom, Maria. But feeling guilty about leaving Chuck, she soon returned to their West Coast home. There she again became the family's breadwinner.

Maria has seen her six-year-old grandson only twice, and then only for a few hours. She isn't allowed to write or visit because her son-in-law blames her for sheltering Candace when she left him temporarily because of his abuse.

When Candace and Chuck first married and lived nearby, the three of them used to pray together regularly. Then Chuck got involved with a group with cult-like teachings and began to control his wife's every move.

Once a year Maria goes out to the West Coast in hopes of seeing her grandchildren. Family and friends join her there in a "prayer drive" around her daughter's home. One couple even walked to the front door to pray. Recently when Chuck learned the dates Maria would be in their area, he moved the family out of their home before she arrived.

As Maria intercedes, standing in the prayer gap for her daughter's family more than three thousand miles away, she is:

1. Praying the spirits manifesting themselves through Chuck will expose themselves to others—perhaps even those in the church he attends—so someone will recognize his need for spiritual help.
2. Praying for her son-in-law to be drawn to repentance and a desire to walk humbly with the Lord, and free his wife from bondage.
3. Praying that her daughter and grandchildren will be given a way of escape until Chuck receives healing.
4. Praying that Candace will remain healthy.
5. Praying for the plan and purpose of God for Candace's life to be released—including all the creative gifts of art, music, and dance that Chuck has squelched.
6. Praying for the family's total freedom and restoration.
7. Enlisting the prayer help of many others who will pray in agreement with her, that God will hasten the deliverance and healing of her daughter's family.

STRATEGY FOR BATTLE

Of course there is no formula for battling for another person in the spiritual realm. The important thing is to seek God's direction in every matter and ask him to reveal the strategy for each specific situation. We recommend our books *A Woman's Guide to Spiritual Warfare* and *The Spiritual Warrior's Prayer Guide* for detailed biblical principles and Scriptures on warfare.

We are told: "Put on the full armor of God so that you can take your stand against the devil's schemes. For our struggle is not against flesh and blood… but against the spiritual forces of evil in the heavenly realms" (Eph 6:11-12).

Put on the armor. If the devil has schemes or devices—military-like strategies—doesn't it seem logical that as Christians we need to ask God for strategies to stand against the enemy's plans? Even a casual reading of the battles fought in the Old Testament reveal that God gave his people a different strategy for each confrontation with their enemies.

Often, in battling for our loved ones we need to come against a stronghold that has them captive. A stronghold is like a fortified castle that you can't seem to penetrate—a place where the enemy's position is most strongly intensified. Spiritually speaking, a stronghold is a mind set or conclusion contrary to Scripture that is firmly entrenched. It is often a thought pattern of hopelessness which causes a person to endure a situation that is clearly contrary to God's Word and God's will.

The apostle Paul explains how our godly weapons can be used against these enemy entrenchments:

> I use God's mighty weapons, not those made by men, to knock down the devil's strongholds. These weapons can break down every proud argument against God and every wall that can be built to keep men from finding him. With these weapons I can capture rebels and bring them back to God, and change them into men whose hearts' desire is obedience to Christ.
>
> **2 Corinthians 10:4-5, LB**

By using your spiritual weapons, which we discuss in various parts of this chapter, you can attack strongholds of deception and unbelief. Following is a warfare prayer you could use for a person who has gotten involved in false doctrine or the occult, for example:

> Father, since it is not your will that any be lost, I bring my loved one Virginia to your throne. With the spiritual weapons you provide, I demolish the stronghold of unbelief, and any inaccurate deduction or deceptive fantasy erected in her mind that has kept her from accepting the true knowledge of Jesus Christ. Lord, by the power of your Holy Spirit, destroy all speculations, arguments, and pretensions so her thoughts will surren-

der in obedience to Jesus, the true Son of God. Thank you for sending Christians across her path—harvesters into the field—to speak into her life the truth about the Lord Jesus. Thank you, Lord, for preparing her heart to receive the truth. Thank you that Virginia's blinders *will come off!* One day she *will confess* Jesus Christ as her Lord. (See 2 Corinthians 10:5 in several translations.)

Prayer through Scripture. Here are some ways to use Scriptures both as a prayer and warfare against the devil. I will paraphrase from the *New American Standard* translation:

Prayer. "God... grant to (name of person) repentance leading to the knowledge of the truth; that he (she) may come to his (her) senses and escape from the snare of the devil, having been held captive by him to do his will." (Remember the prodigal son came to his senses, repented, and came home.) (See 2 Timothy 2:25b, 26.)

Warfare. "Satan, you have held (name of person) captive to do your will, as the Word of God reveals. In the name and authority of Jesus Christ of Nazareth, loose his (her) will so he (she) will be free to accept Jesus as Lord and Savior" (see 2 Timothy 2:25b-26).

Prayer. "Lord, I pray that you will open their eyes and turn them from darkness to light, and from the power of Satan to God, so that they may receive forgiveness of sins, and a place among those who are sanctified by faith in Christ" (see Acts 26:18).

One way to battle in prayer is to use verses of Scripture that fit the situation. Psalm 91 is excellent to pray for protection. How often I've used Psalms 140 and 141, paraphrasing them with names of family members I'm praying for who are being attacked by evil forces. For example:

"Rescue (name of person), O Lord, from evil men; protect him (her) from men of violence, who devise evil plans in their hearts and stir up war every day. They make their tongues as sharp as a serpent's; the poison of vipers is on their lips. Hear, O Lord, my cry for mercy..." (Ps 140:1-3, 6b).

Repent of sin in your own life. A word of caution: you must be sure there is no sin or unforgiveness in your own heart before you battle in the spiritual realm for others. For example, a mother starting to pray for her promiscuous daughter was reminded by the Holy Spirit that she had severely judged her daughter and criticized her lifestyle to other people. She had unforgiveness and bitterness in her heart because the daughter had disappointed her. This mother confessed her sin to God, asked his forgiveness, and then was able to pray for her daughter with a clean heart. In his timing, the Lord will guide her to ask the daughter for forgiveness—that will be the mother's participation in seeing her prayers answered. The goal is not only to see a change in the daughter's lifestyle, but to see reconciliation and healing in their family relationships, and in the daughter's relationship with God.

Paul wrote, "I forgive... for your sakes... in order that no advantage be taken of us by Satan; for we are not ignorant of his schemes" (2 Cor 2:10-11 NASB). Remaining alert and aware of the enemy's schemes is of paramount importance when you're engaged in spiritual warfare.

Fasting. The biblical example of Esther shows us that fasting is one way to help set captives free.

God asks, "Is not this the kind of fasting I have chosen: to loose the chains of injustice and untie the cords of the yoke, to set the oppressed free and break every yoke?" (Is 58:6). Whether we skip one meal a day, or all meals for several days, fasting while praying over a lost loved one helps purify our own heart and sharpens our "hearing ear" to God's direction.

Jesus expected his disciples to fast. Once when they couldn't heal a lunatic boy Jesus said it was "because of your unbelief... This kind goeth not out but by prayer and fasting" (Mt 17:20-21, KJV).

Arthur Wallis in his book *God's Chosen Fast* says:

> The man who prays with fasting is giving heaven notice that he is truly in earnest; that he will not give up nor let God go without the blessing.... You should expect that a season of fasting would prove to be for you, as it was for your Master, a time of conflict with the powers of darkness. Satan will often try to take advantage of your physical condition to launch an attack. Discouragement is one of his weapons. Guard against it by maintaining a spirit of praise.[5]

Agree in prayer with others. While our prayers are powerful (according to James 5:16b), they are even more potent when we pray in agreement with a partner. Jesus encouraged us, "Again, I tell you that if two of you on earth agree about anything you ask for, it will be done for you by my Father in heaven. For where two or three come together in my name, there am I with them" (Mt 18:19-20).

Ask the Lord for the right prayer partner—be it one person or a team—who will agree to pray with you the way God has shown you to pray. Find partners who will pray and remain unwavering until victory is accomplished.

Of course, you must be willing to stand in agreement with them concerning their prayer needs. Paul instructs us, "Carry each other's burdens, and in this way you will fulfill the law of Christ" (Gal 6:2).

WARFARE PRAYER

Following is the prayer which Pastor Stelman H. Smith instructed Nona to pray for her daughter Lorene. You may want to adapt it for your own situation.

Heavenly Father, I ask you in the name and through the blood of the Lord Jesus Christ to rebuke Satan for taking captive that which you created and to build a hedge of thorns around (name of afflicted person). *I pray that by this hedge the influence of all spiritual powers of Satan will be defeated and* (name) *will be protected from spiritual attack. Jesus, I bind Satan and bring all the thoughts in the mind of* (name) *into captivity and to the obedience of the Lord Jesus Christ. I pray that you seal this mind with the blood of the Lord Jesus Christ.*

Also included is the deliverance proclamation for Nona's home which Pastor Smith had her do twice daily:

Satan, by faith I scatter every evil force arrayed against my home, as holy angels smite them in my behalf. Greater is he (Christ) that is with us and more powerful are those with us than those with you. The Father God himself sent his Word to deliver us from your devices (Ps 107:20). I put to flight every demonic power that would harm my family, and bind all false spiritual activity in those I'm praying for (name them all). *I claim victory for them through the shed blood of the Lord Jesus Christ. I've asked God to loose the power of the Holy Spirit in their lives and bind all workings of Satan. Therefore, I break the enemy's hold and spoil his goods in the authority and blood of the Lord Jesus Christ. By faith I invite the peace and power of God the Father, the grace of the Lord Jesus Christ, and the comfort and direction of the Holy Spirit to come and do a great work among our family members—to the glory of the Father, through the Lord Jesus Christ.*

SEVENTEEN

Captive No More

He has sent Me to heal the brokenhearted, to proclaim liberty to the captives, and the opening of the prison to those who are bound. **Isaiah 61:1**

Captive no more! Doesn't that sound wonderful? To walk in victory! The above verse, speaking of the Messiah's mission, was written long before his birth. Early in his ministry Jesus read this prophecy to the people, then proclaimed, "Today this scripture is fulfilled in your hearing" (Lk 4:21). He confirmed that his mission is to set the captives free.

In this book we've shared guidelines for finding freedom from Satan's bondages. But be advised, the enemy will attempt to use weak points and wounds from your past to harass you and diminish your effectiveness. Don't allow this to happen!

As we read about the Israelites preparing to enter and possess the Promised Land, we see God gave Joshua some specifics: "Arise, cross this Jordan, you and all this people, to the land which I am giving to them.... Every place on which the sole of your foot treads, I have given it to you, just as I spoke to Moses" (Jos 1:2b-3, NASB).

Notice the steps:

Arise (get up)
Cross over (start going)
Tread (action necessary—walk)

Whatever enemy territory we must invade to get set free of bondages, it is certain we will have to take the initiative. We have to get up, get going, take action. While the Israelites had a legal right—in the sense of becoming heirs—to the Promised Land, they had to engage the enemy to claim their territory. An attitude of possession was necessary.

POSSESSING OUR FREEDOM

God's promises to us, his children, give us a "legal right" to be free of bondages in our lives. But we have to claim that territory and keep fighting the enemy when he comes to capture us again, whether it's through anger, unforgiveness, torment, harassment, addictions, or hate.

God kept encouraging Joshua: "Be strong and courageous. Do not be terrified; do not be discouraged, for the Lord your God will be with you wherever you go" (Jos 1:9b).

God kept his promise to his people. Unfortunately, the Israelites did not keep their promise to him. They compromised, fell into the sin of idolatry, and thus failed to possess their full inheritance. Idols became obstacles.

Sadly, we have the same tendency. Many believers have allowed God's blessings to become a trap, and they have made idols of their possessions.

LORD, EVERYTHING I OWN IS YOURS

How would you feel to look at a pile of ashes on a concrete slab and realize it was all that remained of your million-dollar, five-bedroom home?

Sandy had been a Christian only two-and-a-half years when her home was destroyed in one of the great California fires in October of 1993. When she made Jesus her Lord a few years earlier she had told him, "Everything I own is yours." After the fire consumed it all, she told him the same thing again.

Frequently women gain a sense of well-being and prestige from their homes. Our homes become an extension of our identity, and many of us acquire a sense of security from our possessions. The loss of those things can be extremely traumatic.

That day, as Sandy ran from the house to her car to escape the fire, she only had time to grab her Bible. Imagine her surprise when she went back later and found her wedding album in the ashes—soaking wet but still salvageable.

She lost everything else—from the Bible her great-grandfather had brought from Sweden in 1868, to all her furniture and household belongings, her clothes, and even some precious jewelry passed on from her grandmother.

"I'd always been a bargain hunter," she admitted. "We had lived in that house for twenty years, and I had too many things. Some of those things can never be replaced—grandmother's jewelry, all the movies and videos, my children's baby pictures—especially the memories! They told me the heat reached seventeen hundred Fahrenheit—it even blew apart our safe. Nothing was saved. But because of this experience I know now that things just aren't that important."

The house was insured and they will rebuild, but the contents of the house were greatly underinsured. On the day of the fire Sandy's reading from her *One Year Bible* spoke about the fall of Babylon: "This is what the Lord Almighty says: Babylon's thick wall will be leveled and her high gates set on fire; the peoples exhaust themselves for nothing, the nation's labor is only fuel for the flames." (Jer 51:58).

When she first entered the evacuation shelter on the day of the fire—not knowing if her house would be standing when she returned—Sandy turned to a Jewish lady beside her and said, "Well, this is like Sodom and Gomorrah—and I will not be like Lot's wife and look back."

"What do you mean?" the lady asked.

"When Lot's wife looked back as her city was burning, she turned to salt," Sandy replied. "None of my possessions is as valuable as my relationship with Jesus Christ. He spared my life, but even if I lost it, I know I would spend eternity with the living God."

"I wish I knew a living God," the lady replied.

Sandy shared more about how she had come to know Jesus and soon led the Jewish woman to accept him as her Messiah.

Does Sandy never grieve over the loss? "Of course, there are nights when I wake up suddenly and remember something very special that was lost, and I get a little sad," she replied. "But then I pray and remind the Lord and myself that those things were really his anyway."

No bondage to possessions in Sandy's life now, for sure.

SINGING TO BARRENNESS

We've mentioned earlier that women can sometimes get "stuck" in their grief so that it becomes a bondage to them. Joanne Smith is a woman who allowed the Lord to help her walk through the steps of grief recovery; then she faced the matter of desiring a new husband. As she prayed about the issue the Lord led her to victory in a unique way.

After four years as a widow, Joanne came upon a biblical approach to the emptiness in her life. She gave us permission to share her story from her book, *How to Say Goodbye:*

> I found that the deep desire in my heart was that I wanted to get married again. I'm not talking about casually whipping off a goal and expecting God to honor it. I spent a lot of time praying about my future and considering all facets of my life. I wrote down the plusses and minuses of singleness and the assets and liabilities of married life. I tried in every way to sort through this list to set my goal for the year. After much prayer, I knew my goal was now to "Meet My Mate in '88."[1]

Then the Lord led her to dig into the meaning of Isaiah 54:1-4, and to sing to her "barrenness." This term not only refers to an inability to bear children; it means unproductive in results, lacking interest or charm, dull and unresponsive. Joanne embraced this broader meaning of the term. She used portions of these verses from *The Amplified Bible* and other translations as the scriptural basis for singing to her barrenness:

> Sing, O barren, you who did not bear; break forth into singing and cry aloud (break out into loud and joyful song). Enlarge your house; build on additions; spread out your home! For you will soon be bursting at the seams!... Do not be afraid; you will not suffer shame. Do not fear disgrace; you will not be humiliated!

She took God at his word and began to sing to the barrenness in her life—"the empty, vacant, bare, bleak, desolate, unfruitful, void areas" and particularly to the "barrenness in my bed," she said. Because many of the psalms are prayers set to music, she sang her prayers too, no matter how foolish it may have seemed.

> I sang gratefully, untiringly, consistently, tearfully, triumphantly, with lots of faith and with only a glimmer of hope. I sang in the morning, in the evening, and in the middle of the night. I sang when I felt like it, and I sang when I could barely get out the words.[2]

Joanne also taught those in her grief recovery classes how to sing to their barren areas, demonstrating it as a method of prayer. Soon she began receiving reports from people who were experiencing answers to prayer as they sang to their barren places. Yet she had not seen even a glimmer of her "Mr. Right." She writes:

> When I was all alone and uncertain about my future, I chose to sing instead of letting the enemy defeat me. I sang to God in all

> areas of my barrenness—health problems, relationship challenges, and financial problems. I simply opened my mouth and used any combination of tones or an old familiar tune. I sang, "God, I'm barren in energy. I ask you to give me fruitfulness in this area. I praise you, Lord, for I know you are faithful to give me strength and vitality.[3]

She was encouraged as she read about the power of Paul and Silas' song in prison; it caused an earthquake that shook the prison and freed all those there (see Acts 16:25-26). So she kept on singing—even intensified her song. Some areas of her life were so barren she said she had to sing with much determination until she had peace.

She had begun singing in January 1988 about a potential mate. For months she sang on. In September she met Irv Bloom, a widower. By the middle of the next year, he proposed. They have been happily singing together for several years now as husband and wife. "God really answered my prayer in a wonderful way," Joanne told Quin.

While her example of praying and singing was for her own needs, Pastor Jack Hayford leads his congregation in singing over their city to see spiritual breakthroughs. Others are beginning to follow his example. The point is this: whatever strategy the Lord gives you in prayer, if it lines up with the Word of God, that is the tactic to use for that particular battle, or to break a particular bondage.

LAUGHTER AND SHOUTING

When the Lord frees you—a captive one—your mouth will be filled with laughter and joyful shouting. One definition of laughter includes "joy restored" and "a mark of gratification."

Consider how the Jews expressed their overwhelming joy when they returned from Babylonian captivity after seventy years in exile: "When the Lord brought back the captive ones of Zion, we were like those who dream. Then our mouth was filled with laughter, and our tongue with joyful shouting" (Ps 126:1-2a, NASB).

Paul wrote, "Rejoice in the Lord always. I will say it again: Rejoice!" (Phil 4:4). In the Bible, women who rejoiced are Miriam, Hannah, and Mary. King David gave praise to God seven times a day. Daniel, who prayed three times a day while he was in captivity, also gave thanks.[4] One of the most liberating things you can do—even before your victory is complete—is to walk in praise, rejoicing, and laughter.

Many biblical references to laughter mean "to mock, to make sport, to deride, to laugh, to scorn"—a very appropriate stance to take toward Satan, even before you are completely free. Scripture records that God laughs at the enemy!

"The One enthroned in heaven laughs; the Lord scoffs at them" (Ps 2:4). "The wicked plot against the righteous and gnash their teeth at them; but the Lord laughs at the wicked, for he knows their day is coming" (Ps 37:12-13).

So you can laugh, sing, or shout your way to victory!

TWELVE STEPS OUT?

A well-known recovery plan called the Twelve Step Program, first developed by Alcoholics Anonymous, is sometimes adapted for use in counseling programs dealing with a variety of problems.

Following the Twelve Steps can be an important beginning to help you get on the road to a healthier life. Yet we feel they contain pitfalls we should not ignore—notably the step which advocates turning one's life over to the care of "God as we understand him." We share the concerns expressed in Dr. John White's evaluation:

> All of them [the Twelve Steps] reflect biblical teaching.... Nevertheless, I believe they are incomplete Bible teaching, and

> at one point they are seriously watered down. The founders of AA knew this. They were not pretending to invent what are actually very ancient principles. But they also knew who they were trying to reach—men and women for whom the very word God had bitter associations, who resented certain people who quoted God while at the same time shunning them.
>
> ... If you turn your life over to your own concept of God, how do you know whether that concept is powerful enough? No, if I am to turn my life over to a God, it must be God as he is. Not God as I conceive him, but God as he conceives himself to be. If there is a God, then he is a person, not an idea. He is not something I have made up out of my own understanding.[5]

He goes on to say that for repentance to take place we must realize that our own resolution cannot bring about lasting change. We need divine illumination to see ourselves as we really are. Admitting helplessness is the first step toward real and lasting change.

Following is Dr. White's ten-step modification of AA's program:

1. I face the fact, and tell God I now know that I am helpless. I tell him I need to see clearly.
2. I tell God I need to see my own inner nature as well as his greatness and his kindness. I accept his promise to show me all I need to see.
3. I offer my body as a living sacrifice to God, and as an act of worship.
4. In repentance I ask God to search my heart by praying Psalm 139:23-24. I promise God: "As you do so, I will write down those sins and failures to which you draw my attention."
5. God helping me, I will admit to myself, to God, and also to a friend the exact nature of my sins. Give me a friend to whom I may be accountable.

6. Lord, I want to be entirely ready for you to remove every sinful tendency in me. So far as I know, I am ready. But go on testing me, showing me where my motives are phony.
7. I know you are willing to forgive me, but I ask you to make your forgiveness clear in the deepest parts of my being and not just in my intellect. Show me I am forgiven indeed. Show me the love of Christ as shown on the cross.
8. I will make a list of people I have hurt and wronged, beginning with those closest to me. I face before God my responsibility to act.
9. Wherever I can, I will make amends, and do so as soon as possible.
10. God, I resolve to come before you at certain special times to let you examine my heart and life.[6]

GETTING FREE IS A PROCESS

Perhaps the most important truth in these steps is that *they are steps.* In other words, achieving freedom is very often a process, not just an event. Sometimes we escape bondage as instantly as being released from handcuffs. Other times it is as gradual as finding your way out of a jungle or a maze. It is important to take steps!

We see in Scripture this pattern for growing into maturity in Christ:

> Jesus has the power of God. His power has given us everything we need to live and to serve God. We have these things because we know him. Jesus called us by his glory and goodness. Through his glory and goodness he gave us the very great and rich gifts he promised us. With those gifts you can share in being like God. And the world will not ruin you with its evil desires.

> Because you have these blessings, you should try as much as you can to add these things to your lives: to your faith, add goodness; and to your goodness, add knowledge; and to your knowledge, add self-control; and to your self-control, add the ability to hold on; and to your ability to hold on, add service for God; and to your service for God, add kindness for your brothers and sisters in Christ; and to this kindness, add love. If all these things are in you and are growing, they will help you never to be useless. They will help your knowledge of our Lord Jesus Christ make your lives better. **2 Peter 1:3-8, NCV**

SPEAK TO YOUR MOUNTAIN

To get free and stay free—to be captive no more—I (Quin) have learned a valuable lesson from these words of Jesus:

> "Have faith in God," Jesus answered. "I tell you the truth, if anyone says to this mountain, 'Go, throw yourself into the sea,' and does not doubt in his heart but believes that what he says will happen, it will be done for him. Therefore I tell you, whatever you ask for in prayer, believe that you have received it, and it will be yours. And when you stand praying, if you hold anything against anyone, forgive him, so that your Father in heaven may forgive you your sins." **Mark 11:22-25**

We see two keys here: believe that your prayers will be answered, and forgive if you want them answered. Sometimes the enemy looms as big as a mountain in our lives. But I'm learning to speak to my mountain. I address the problem, circumstance, or bondage, as Jesus did: "Mountain, move!"

I heard this slogan from missionary Wayne Myers and a friend has made a cross-stitch hanging of it for my prayer room wall:

> Don't tell God how big your mountain is…
> Tell your mountain how big God is.

You may see your bondage as overwhelming, utterly impossible. I'm sure those Israelites who had been wandering in the wilderness for forty years wondered if they would ever see the Promised Land and victory!

God is a mountain-mover. But he needs our cooperation. We must want to be free. We must be willing to take the steps necessary to get free. We must settle in our hearts that he alone is the bondage-breaker.

VICTORY SHOUT

"Through and with God we shall do valiantly, for He it is Who shall tread down our adversaries" (Ps 108:13, AMPLIFIED). Lord, we praise you for the victories you will lead us through! Thank you for setting the captives free!

NOTES

ONE
What Is Bondage? How Does It Occur?

1. Arthur Penrhyn Stanley, ***The Epistles of St. Paul to the Corinthians*** (Minneapolis, Minn.: Klock & Klock, 1981 reprint of 1858 edition), 71.
2. Dean Sherman, ***Spiritual Warfare for Every Christian*** (Seattle, Wash.: Frontline Communications, 1990), 107.
3. Tom White, ***Breaking Strongholds*** (Ann Arbor, Mich.: Servant, 1993), 38.

TWO
God Wants You Free

1. Joseph Henry Thayer, ***A Greek-English Lexicon of the New Testament*** (Grand Rapids, Mich.: Baker, 1977), 384.
2. Max Lucado, ***No Wonder They Call Him the Savior*** (Portland, Ore.: Multnomah, 1986), 36-37.

THREE
The Bondage of Grief and Disappointment

1. C.S. Lewis, ***A Grief Observed*** (New York: Seaburn, 1961), 7-8.
2. Joanne Smith and Judy Biggs, ***How to Say Goodbye*** (Lynnwood, Wash.: Aglow, 1990), 57-58. For grief seminars, contact Joanne Smith Bloom at 503-771-4341 (Portland, Ore.).
3. Barbara Johnson, ***Pack Up Your Gloomies in a Great Big Box, Then Sit on the Lid and Laugh!*** (Dallas, Tex.: Word, 1993), 32.

FOUR
Anger That Imprisons

1. William Barclay, *The Letters to the Galatians and Ephesians*, rev. ed. (Philadelphia, Pa.: Westminster, 1976), 156.
2. H. Norman Wright, *Questions Women Ask in Private* (Ventura, Calif.: Regal, 1993), 235-36.
3. David Wilkerson, "Tame Your Tongue," from the *Times Square Church Pulpit Series*, February 7, 1994.
4. Psalm 141:3.

FIVE
The Bondage of Selfish Ambition

1. "Daughters of Murphy Brown," *Newsweek*, August 2, 1993, 58.
2. Mabel Williamson, *Have We No Rights?* (Chicago, Ill.: Moody, 1957), 126.

SIX
Freedom from Rejection and Abuse

1. Wright, 243.
2. Nancy Groom, *From Bondage to Bonding* (Colorado Springs, Colo.: Navpress, 1991), 89.
3. Grace Ketterman, *Verbal Abuse: Healing the Hidden Wound* (Ann Arbor, Mich.: Servant, 1992), 14.
4. Rolf Garborg, *The Family Blessing* (Dallas, Tex.: Word, 1990), 32.
5. Philippians 1:6.

SEVEN
Freedom from Shame and Guilt

1. Pia Mellody, *Facing Codependence* (New York, N.Y.: HarperCollins, 1989), 94-98.
2. Mellody, 99-100.
3. Adapted from seminar material by Pia Mellody.
4. A. W. Tozer, *The Best of A.W. Tozer* compiled by Warren W. Wiersbe, (Harrisburg, Pa.: Christian Publications, 1978), 121-22.
5. Adapted from a testimony appearing in *The Scribe*, Church of the King newsletter, Dallas, August-September 1993.

EIGHT
Fear vs. Trust

1. *Spirit Filled Life Bible,* NKJV, (Nashville, Tenn.: Thomas Nelson, 1991), footnote on p. 1415.
2. Fred Smith, "Wait to Worry," *The Christian Reader,* published by *Christianity Today,* June 1993, 53.
3. Fred Smith, 56.

NINE
Family Ties That Bind

1. *The E.W. Bullinger Companion Bible* (Grand Rapids, Mich.: Zondervan, 1964), appendix 44. iv.
2. Quin Sherrer and Ruthanne Garlock, *A Woman's Guide to Spiritual Warfare* (Ann Arbor, Mich.: Servant, 1991), 109.
3. Catherine Marshall, *Something More* (Carmel, N.Y.: Guideposts Associates edition, 1974), 62-63.
4. Marshall, 63.
5. Marshall, 67-68.
6. David and Sharon Sneed, *Understanding Your Family Chemistry* (Ann Arbor, Mich.: Servant, 1992), 52.
7. Sneed and Sneed, 50.

TEN
The Bondage of Addictions

1. Archibald D. Hart, *Healing Life's Hidden Addictions* (Ann Arbor, Mich.: Servant, 1990), 193, 195.
2. "Shopping Addicts Buying Trouble," by Harry Wessel (Knight Ridder-Tribune News Wire), *The Dallas Morning News,* January 11, 1994.
3. Hart, 19.

ELEVEN
Untwisting Sexuality

1. Andrew Comiskey, *Pursuing Sexual Wholeness* (Lake Mary, Fla.: Creation House, 1989), 37.
2. Jane Johnson Struck, "Is God's Love 'One Size Fits All'?" (interview with Liz Curtis Higgs), *Today's Christian Woman,* January-February 1994, 82-83.

3. Ingrid Trobisch, *The Joy of Being a Woman* (San Francisco, Calif.: Harper Row, 1975), 3-4.
4. John White, *Eros Defiled: The Christian Sexual Sin* (Downers Grove, Ill.: InterVarsity Press, 1977), 11.
5. Taken from "In Defense of a Little Virginity," newspaper ad by Focus on the Family, Colorado Springs, Colo.
6. Michael Cavanaugh, *God's Call to the Single Adult* (Springdale, Pa.: Whitaker, 1986), 68.
7. Judy Reamer, *Feelings Women Rarely Share* (Springdale, Pa.: Whitaker, 1987), 51.
8. Reamer, 144-45.
9. John White, *Eros Defiled*, 44.
10. Prayer based on 1 Thessalonians 5:22-23.

TWELVE
The Bondage of Satan's Counterfeits

1. *Dallas Morning News*, January 15, 1994.
2. Michael Green, *Exposing the Prince of Darkness* (Ann Arbor, Mich.: Servant, 1991), 149-50, 185.
3. Charles H. Kraft, *Defeating Dark Angels* (Ann Arbor, Mich.: Servant, 1992), 27, 66-67.
4. *Webster's New Collegiate Dictionary* (Springfield, Mass.: G.C. Merriam, 1974), 794.
5. *The Watchman Expositor* (P.O. Box 13340, Arlington, Tex. 76094), Vol. 10, No. 9, 1993, 3.
6. *The Watchman Expositor*, 4.
7. Herbert Lockyer, general editor, *Nelson's Illustrated Bible Dictionary* (Nashville, Tenn.: Thomas Nelson, 1986), 115.

THIRTEEN
What Happens When You Don't Forgive

1. Matthew 18:21-35.
2. Herbert Lockyer, *All the Parables of the Bible* (Grand Rapids, Mich.: Zondervan, 1963), 219.

FOURTEEN
Forgiving Sets You Free

1. H. Norman Wright, *Always Daddy's Girl* (Ventura, Calif.: Regal, 1989), 235-36.

FIFTEEN
Developing Spiritual Discernment

1. Tom White, ***The Believer's Guide to Spiritual Warfare*** (Ann Arbor, Mich.: Servant, 1990), 91.
2. Dean Sherman, 42-43.
3. Tom White, ***The Believer's Guide to Spiritual Warfare***, 105.
4. Herman Riffel, ***Your Dreams: God's Neglected Gift*** (Lincoln, Va.: Chosen, 1981), 124.

SIXTEEN
Helping Family and Friends Break Free

1. C. Peter Wagner, ***Warfare Prayer*** (Ventura, Calif.: Regal, 1992), 61-62.
2. ***Spirit Filled Life Bible***, 1436, footnote.
3. Elizabeth Alves, ***The Mighty Warrior*** (Bulverde, Tex.: Canopy), 145.
4. Judson Cornwall, ***Praying the Scriptures*** (Lake Mary, Fla.: Creation House, 1990), 212-13.
5. Arthur Wallis, ***God's Chosen Fast*** (Fort Washington, Pa.: Christian Literature Crusade, 1968), 42, 86.

SEVENTEEN
Captive No More

1. Smith and Biggs, 152.
2. Smith and Biggs, 153.
3. Smith and Biggs, 154.
4. Exodus 15:20-21; 1 Samuel 2:1-10; Luke 1:46-55; Psalm 119:164; Daniel 6:10.
5. John White, ***Changing on the Inside*** (Ann Arbor, Mich.: Servant, 1991), 152, 158.
6. John White, ***Changing on the Inside***, adapted from pp. 156-76.

ABOUT THE AUTHORS

Quin Sherrer earned her B.S. in journalism at Florida State University and has a background as feature writer for newspapers and numerous Christian magazines. She's the author of *How to Pray for Your Children,* an Aglow best-seller for several years now published in eight languages. She and Ruthanne Garlock coauthored *How to Forgive Your Children, How to Pray for Family and Friends, A Woman's Guide to Spiritual Warfare,* and *The Spiritual Warrior's Prayer Guide.* Quin and Laura Watson coauthored *A House of Many Blessings.*

Quin, a winner of the *Guideposts Magazine* Writer's Contest, was also named Writer of the Year for the 1990 Florida Christian Writer's In Touch Conference.

She has traveled extensively in the United States and abroad in the past nine years speaking on her book topics and encouraging audiences with "how-tos" for praying more effectively for their families. She has appeared on more than sixty radio and television programs including the *700 Club*, CBN's *Heart to Heart,* Trinity Broadcasting Network, and *100 Huntley Street.*

As a member of both the international and United States boards of Women's Aglow Fellowship, she is often a keynote speaker at Aglow retreats and conferences.

Quin and her husband LeRoy, a retired NASA engineer, have been married thirty-eight years and are parents of three adult children. They currently live in Colorado Springs, Colorado, where they are active at Springs Harvest Fellowship.

Ruthanne Garlock is a Bible teacher and author from Dallas, Texas with a varied background in international ministry. She is married to John Garlock, a Bible instructor at Christ For The Nations Institute in Dallas.

For four years they worked with a Bible school in Brussels, Belgium, teaching ministerial students from Europe and the Middle East. Together the two have traveled and taught in leadership training seminars in the United States and more than thirty countries on five continents. Each year they spend several months as guest teachers at overseas Bible schools and pastors' seminars.

This is the fifth title she has coauthored with Quin Sherrer (the list is at the front of the book). She also headed up the editing team to abridge *The Christian*

in Complete Armour, a seventeenth-century treatise on spiritual warfare by English pastor William Gurnall (published by Banner of Truth in three volumes). Prayer and spiritual warfare are subjects about which she often teaches for seminars and retreats.

Ruthanne holds a B.A. in religious education from Central Bible College, Springfield, Missouri. She serves on the boards of Christian Haitian Outreach, an orphanage ministry in Haiti, and Intercessors International, a prayer ministry based in Texas. The Garlocks have three adult children and four grandchildren.